Jeeves, I Need Help!

ALSO FROM ASK JEEVES FOR KIDS

Jeeves, I'm Bored: 25 Internet Adventures for Kids

Jeeves, I Need Help!

TIPS AND TRICKS FOR KIDS ON THE NET

CALLIE GREGORY
WITH LYNDA GREENE

Illustrations by
Marcos Sorensen

ASK JEEVES • EMERYVILLE, CALIFORNIA

ASK JEEVES is a federally registered trademark and service mark of Ask Jeeves, Inc., ASK JEEVES FOR KIDS is a federally registered trademark and service mark of Ask Jeeves, Inc.

Copyright © 2000 by Ask Jeeves, Inc. Illustrations © 2000 by Ask Jeeves, Inc.

Published by Ask Jeeves, Inc. All rights reserved. No part of this book may be used or reproduced in any manner whatsoever without written permission of the publisher, except in the case of brief quotations embodied in critical articles or reviews. Address requests for permission to Ask Jeeves, Attention: Book Permissions Department, 5858 Horton Street, Emeryville, CA 94608, E-mail: Books@askjeeves.com.

"Cracks on the Ocean Floor" by Lucy Lehrer in SCHOLASTIC NEWS ZONE, Scholastic Web site. Copyright © 2000 by Scholastic Inc. Reprinted by permission.

As far as we know, the addresses and descriptions of Web sites in this book were correct at the time the book was printed. If you find something that needs to be changed, please let us know so we can fix it the next time we go to press. We'd also love to hear what you think of the book. Send comments and corrections to *Books@askjeeves.com*.

Note to parents: This book includes online and offline activities for children. The publisher and the author have made every reasonable effort to ensure that the activities are safe when performed as instructed but assume no responsibility for any damage caused or sustained while performing the activities in this book. Parents, guardians, and/or teachers should supervise young readers who undertake the activities in this book.

ISBN: 1-930108-02-8

Library of Congress Catalog Number: 00-134466

Design by Seventeenth Street Studios

Distributed in the United States by Publishers Group West

Distributed in Canada by Raincoast Books

Printed in the United States of America

10 9 8 7 6 5 4 3 2 1

Developed and Managed by Melissa Schwarz

To Mom and Dad for encouraging me with their secret tips and tricks on life
—*C. G.*

Contents

Jeeves to the Rescue! 1

Part I Jeeves, I Need School Help! 5

Chapter 1 Cast Your Net 6
  If you need help...
  Picking a subject
  Researching a topic
  Gathering information

Chapter 2 Be Exact 15
  If you need help...
  Answering a question
  Finding a fact
  Confirming a detail

Chapter 3 Consider the Source 24
  If you need help...
  Evaluating sources
  Finding reliable references
  Creating a bibliography

Chapter 4 Get the Picture 33
  If you need help...
  Writing a report, poem, or journal
  Completing a project
  Illustrating your work

Chapter 5 Ask an Expert 39
  If you need help...
  Getting online homework help
  Answering a tricky question
  Understanding a concept

Chapter 6 Use the News 46
  If you need help...
  Tracking a current event
  Gathering the latest information
  Reporting your story

Part II Jeeves, I Need Life Help! 53

Chapter 7 Make Contact 54
  If you need help...
  Connecting with friends
  Meeting new people
  Joining online discussions

Chapter 8 Take a Break 60
  If you need help...

Exploring an interest
Developing a hobby
Trading experiences with others

Chapter 9 Get Creative 65
If you need help...
Developing creative skills
Sharing your creations
Getting useful feedback

Chapter 10 Seek Advice 73
If you need help...
Dealing with friends and family
Answering a health question
Solving a problem

Part III Jeeves, I Need to Know! **79**

Chapter 11 Search Engines Built for Kids 81

Chapter 12 Collecting Information 83

Chapter 13 Follow the Peas and Cues (or Netiquette) 87

Chapter 14 Safety Net: Protect Yourself While Surfing 89

Chapter 15 How to Can Spam 94

Glossary On Your Terms 98

Jeeves to the Rescue!

Sure, you need help online, but who is Jeeves, and how can he make a difference? Quite simply, Jeeves is your Internet butler, and he's standing by at *www.ajkids.com*.

Get What You Need ... Fast!

Anytime day or night, Jeeves goes to work on your questions and quandaries. All you have to do is ask. Jeeves will introduce you to people, places, and information on the Web that can make your life run a little more smoothly. He'll track down answers to history questions, find examples of book reports, and give you a helping hand to create your own works of art.

How can one butler do all that? Jeeves lives on the Internet, so he knows where to find what you need. He'll pick out the best resources the Net has to offer so you can use them in your own world. Jeeves is ready to ride! He's just waiting for a visit from you.

How to Use This Book

Everyone comes to the Internet with different needs at different times. That's why this book is divided into three sections. You choose whether you need help with school, help with life, or help with understanding Net basics, like online safety.

The book doesn't have to be read in any particular order. Look over the table of contents and dive into the chapter that comes closest to matching your situation or interests. When you see what you're looking for, read on.

TIME-SAVER TIPS. Throughout this book, Jeeves offers you Time-Saver Tips about the Internet—ways you can use time to your best advantage. Check out the simple suggestions to sharpen your Internet IQ.

KEEP YOUR EYE OUT FOR ICONS. Each of the three sections in the book is represented by a unique *icon*, or symbol. The icons tell you that more information about a subject can be found in another section.

 Jeeves, I Need School Help

 Jeeves, I Need Life Help

 Jeeves, I Need to Know

LEARN TO TALK THE TALK. Terms in *italics* help you understand how the Internet works. If you're not familiar with an italicized term—even if you're not sure you know exactly what it means—turn to the glossary on page 98 for a brief explanation.

👁 **REMEMBER, TIMES CHANGE.** *Web sites* can morph overnight. So don't be surprised if a Web site referred to in this book or in a search *results* list changes dramatically or even disappears. On the other hand, fantastic new sites are added all the time. You can rely on Jeeves to help you find the latest sites about your subject. In the meantime, if you try to go to a Web site and you get a message that the site is unavailable, try back a little later or use another *browser*. The site or your browser could be busy or have technical problems.

A note about addresses: When you see a *Web site address,* or *URL,* in this book, keep in mind that all Internet addresses start with the prefix *http://* and in most cases (but not all) the letters *www* follow. When you see a Web address in this book that starts with *www.,* you may need to add the prefix *http://* when you type the address into your computer. Otherwise, type the address exactly as you see it here.

Searching High and Low

By now you've probably heard so many promises about the power of technology, you might think that the World Wide Web—and Jeeves, the Internet butler—can wash your clothes, iron them, fold them, and put them away for you.

The truth is, even with the best computer in the world, you will still have to do most of the work yourself. Worried? Don't be. This book tells you all you need to know to use tools called *search engines*. Search engines probe the Web to find information and sites that might be useful to you. They are free. All you have to do is tell them what you need.

Ask Jeeves for Kids—online at *www.ajkids.com*—is a special search engine that lets you ask a question in your own words, like **How do robots work?** Jeeves thinks over your question and comes back with *matching questions* and *metasearch results,* lists of resources to help you find the answer. You click the best match for what you want to know.

You can also track down information using *keywords,* that is, words that describe the subject you're searching for, such as **robots** or **kids' clothes.** When you type in keywords at other search engines for kids—such as *www.searchopolis.com, www.yahooligans.com,* and *www.lycoszone.com*—you'll get a list of related Web sites to explore.

Hey, wait a minute. Maybe all those promises about technology aren't so far-fetched after all! There very well could be a way to use the Internet to help you manage your laundry chores. Armed with Jeeves' tips and tricks, maybe you'll be able to invent a robot to do it all!

What's the difference between Ask Jeeves for Kids at *www.ajkids.com* and Jeeves' general site at *www.ask.com*? Turn to Chapter 11, "Search Engines Built for Kids," and find out.

PART ONE

Jeeves, I Need School Help!

An Internet butler's job is never done. School creates so many reasons to use the Internet that kids are constantly coming to Jeeves for help. If you have access to the Web and its resources, Jeeves can help you use it to your advantage. He can't promise you A's and B's, but he can guide you and cheer for you so you can do your best.

This section goes to the heart of your homework challenges, but it's not meant to add to your load. Cruise through it at your own pace and don't worry if you don't pick up every tidbit of information you see. Let your intuition and imagination do the driving. If you stall and need a jumpstart along the way, or want more directions, you can always go to www.ajkids.com and flag down Jeeves.

CHAPTER 1

Cast Your Net

- -

If you need help...

☞ Picking a subject
☞ Researching a topic
☞ Gathering information

Start Here

If you can imagine a subject, you can find out about it on the Internet. It's that simple.

Whether you're choosing a subject for a report (one that interests you *and* that your teacher will accept for an assignment), or you have a topic and you're ready to get rolling on research, the Web is a great place to look. You can go all out—cast your net wide on the Net!—then keep only the prize finds that help you with your project. You want the right sites—those that have information you

understand and can use. With tips from Jeeves, you'll learn to quickly look through a wide variety of sites and pick out the ones that are right for you.

Think Big

Pencil and paper might seem old-fashioned, but if you don't have a clue which topic you want to research, they're the perfect tools to start with. Jot down a list of categories that appeal to you before launching into the World Wide Web. Doing this will give you a big lead on your search. Brainstorm the possibilities and list as many as you can come up with. Laser beams. Baseball Hall of Fame. Civil War. Bread mold. You name it. It's your list, and it's time to think big. Once you have a list, read through it and put a checkmark by your favorite topics. Now it's time to go to the Web.

Discovery and Surprise

One fun thing about doing research on the Internet is that you never know for sure what you'll find. Or what you'll find interesting. Did your teacher ask for a report on a famous mountain? You can be hot on a search about Mt. Everest when you come across a cool site about the volcano Mt. Etna. All of a sudden your interest flips from the extreme cold of Everest's harsh heights to the fiery core of Etna's explosive peak. That's how easy it is to run hot and cold on the World Wide Web!

Start your exploration by logging on to the Internet and opening your *browser* software. Type in the *URL*, or *Web site address*, for a *search engine*. Search engines take your questions or *keywords* and go out and crawl around the Web to find sites that match your needs.

Use the following strategies to start your research:

👁 **ASK A QUESTION.** Go to Ask Jeeves for Kids at *www.ajkids.com* and type your question in the box. For the best results, ask a simple, direct question. For example, let's say you have an assignment to write a description of any place in the world and why you would want to go there. If you know you want to go to Africa, but don't know exactly where, ask Jeeves, **Where can I find out more about Africa?** Click the *matching questions* and *metasearch results*. The Web pages you find will give you lots of ideas for places to write about.

👁 **USE KEYWORDS.** This is the time to be open to possibilities. But even with a wide topic you'll want to create boundaries for your search. Go to *ajkids.com* or the home page of another kid search engine, such as *www.yahooligans.com*, and type in keywords about your topic. For a science project about how airplanes fly, you could simply type **airplanes** and click SEARCH. On *yahooligans.com*, you'll find links to more airplane sites than you could ever visit, at least before your assignment is due. If you already know you want to build a unique paper airplane for your science project, narrow your search by typing **paper airplanes**.

👁 **TRY DIFFERENT SEARCH ENGINES.** To fully explore a topic, conduct your search using more than one search engine. Each one will give you different results. See page 82 for a list of search engines.

Spell Write

Jeeves doesn't want to be a stickler, but when you type a question or *key-*

words for him—or keywords for other search engines—you want to make sure your spelling is correct so you get the best results.

If you misspell a word in a question for Jeeves, you will get a *link* that says I THINK YOU MAY HAVE MISSPELLED SOMETHING. Click this link, and tell Jeeves which word you meant by choosing it from the list provided.

If you find that you often misspell words in your questions, ask Jeeves, **Where can I get help with spelling?** Or look up words you're not sure of at *www.m-w.com/dictionary.htm*

Gude luk ande happie spelng!

Case Closed

When you type a question or *keyword* into a *search engine*, you don't have to worry about which letters to capitalize. You can use all lowercase letters ... or MiX iT uP! To a search engine, upper- and lowercase letters look just the same.

Question the Question

Like any accommodating butler, Jeeves is ready to serve you in whatever way he can. But it's up to you to tell him what you want him to find. If you go to *www.ajkids.com* and ask Jeeves, **Where can I find out about rock climbing?**, he might bring back results leading to sites about rocks, sites about climbing, and sites about rock climbing.

Each word you include in a question for Jeeves increases the possibilities for the response. You will get different results if you ask, **Where can I find out about rock climbing in Yosemite National Park?** Try it yourself and see what happens. Get ready to rock 'n' roll!

Keyword Workout

Try this exercise and see how different keywords affect your search results. You can bulk up or trim down by flexing your word power.

Go to *www.searchopolis.com* and take these steps:

1. Type **sports** in the box and click Go. Under the tab files you'll see the number of Web pages found. Record your findings here. Number of Web sites found: _____.

2. Now use two words about the same subject. Type **water polo** and click Go. Number of Web sites found: _____.

3. Now use three words about the same subject. Type **water polo rules** and click Go. Number of Web sites found: _____.

What happened? Which set of *results* gives you the best chance of finishing your homework this century? You do the math! Put your homework assignment through your own keyword workout to get your results into great shape.

Three's a Charm

You've probably heard the expression "good things come in threes." Some people even think *bad* things happen in threes. Whatever the folklore about the number three, the truth is, you can find strength in numbers.

Sometimes your teacher will give you a set number of ideas or facts to communicate in your assignment. Often you will have to support those ideas or facts by using more than one source, as well. Look at your topic from all sorts of angles to see if there are three or more ideas for you to develop. If not, you might want to find another subject that gives you more to think about. You might even find the best subject—on your third try!

List Toppers

The Little Search Engine That Could (which is to say most *search engines*) will rank your *results* by how well they match your request. When you ask a question at *ajkids.com*, the question at the top of the list will be the one Jeeves thinks is closest to your original question. Other search engines try to list the most useful results at the top, too. The list will rank results from the most likely to fit your *keyword* description to the least likely. Use this ranking to your advantage and check out links at the top of the list first.

Idea Scout — If you don't know which topic you want to research, open a few books and scan the table of contents and index in each one for inspiration.

Say you have a language arts assignment to write about a specific time in history. Go to the front or the back of your social studies book and read through the list of subjects covered. Read more about subjects that sound appealing—even the ones you haven't studied in class yet. Choose the most interesting one, then go to Ask Jeeves for Kids at *ajkids.com* to get more information for your report.

Are you curious about the Nez Percé people? Reading about this subject in a history book or encyclopedia will give you ideas for a few questions to ask Jeeves. Or you could simply ask, **Who are the Nez Percé?** In the end, not only will you have a great subject for your language arts class, but you'll already know about the Nez Percé when the subject rolls around later in social studies.

Big-Time Scan

Imagine reading every word of every site on the Web. You might find a lot of interesting material but still not be any closer to finishing the homework assignment due tomorrow. One of the most important skills you can learn as an Internet researcher is *scanning*. Scanning just means looking over a Web site to see if it has what you need.

Use these scanning strategies:

- 👁 Look over the descriptions of the first 5 to 10 results of your search. Remember: They are listed with the closest matches at the top. Pick your first choice.

- 👁 Read the headlines on the Web page.

- 👁 Notice the highlighted or underlined words that stand out as *links*. They can help you summarize a site's content.

- 👁 Click the *site map*, if there is one, and read it over.

Do you see information you can use? If so, click on a few of the links and keep reading. If not, go back to your search *results* and click on your next choice.

When you find a site with lots of information you can use, keep track of the *URL* so you can include it in your resource list or bibliography. To find out more, see Chapter 3, "Consider the Source." (PAGE 24)

Did you find some Web pages that were just perfect for what you're doing? Don't let 'em slip away! Find out how to scoop 'em up—now! See Chapter 12, "Collecting Information." (PAGE 83)

Two-Minute Scan Slam

Put your eyeballs and your memory to the test with this scanning exercise. Try it on your own or with a friend. Have a piece of paper and a pen or pencil handy.

1. *On your mark*—Go to www.nationalgeographic.com (don't peek!)
2. *Get set*—Set a kitchen timer for two minutes or get your friend to watch the clock for you.
3. *Go!*—Look over the site to find out as much as you can about it. Remember those scanning strategies!
4. *Stop!*—When the buzzer goes off, close the Web page and write down everything you can remember about what you saw. Now put your paper aside and time your friend, or time yourself again.
5. *Test yourself*—Can you and your friend answer these questions without looking at the site again?

   Does the site have a map or index?

   Is there a kids' link?

   What was the lead headline?

   What were some of the other stories about?

Practice the two-minute scan slam on other sites and watch your scanning skills get sharper.

CHAPTER 2

Be Exact

If you need help...

- Answering a question
- Finding a fact
- Confirming a detail

Start Here

The clock is ticking, you're tired, and you want to finish your homework quickly. This is no time to fool around. You have to find one important fact to put in your report. Where do you begin?

When you need to answer a specific question or track down a detail, the World Wide Web can seem like a mighty big place. Your challenge is to get *specific*. You have to sort through a lot of information to find just the right fact. Now is the time to jump on the *search engine* express and take a nonstop ride to choice *Web sites* that will answer your question.

Get to the Point

Log on to the Internet, open your *browser* software, and type in *www.ajkids.com* to get to Ask Jeeves for Kids. Or go to one of the other *search engines* that are ready, willing, and able to work for you (see page 81).

Use the following strategies to search for the fact you need:

- **ASK A QUESTION.** When you go to Jeeves for help, you can ask a question in the natural way you would ask a teacher or a parent. For instance, **How many planets are in our solar system?** or **What are the rules for using hands in soccer?** Just type your question in the box provided. For the best results, ask a simple, direct question. For example, type **Where is my funnybone?** and then click Ask.

    Jeeves will respond with a list of *matching questions* and *meta-search results*. Follow your fact-finding instincts to choose the match you think has the best chance of giving you the answer. If you don't find your answer at the first *Web site*, click the Back button on your *browser* to go back to the Jeeves results list and click your second choice. If you still don't find the answer, try wording your question another way for a new search to see if you get better results. One way to reword a question is to change how you describe your topic. That is, if the question **What causes baldness?** doesn't lead to an answer, you could ask, **Why do people lose their hair?** If you don't find an answer to a specific question like **What time is it in Australia?** you can ask, **Where can I find the time zones of the world?** Rewording questions gets easier the more you practice.

- **USE SPECIFIC KEYWORDS.** When looking for facts on the Internet, you can save a lot of time just by using good *keywords*. Go to *ajkids.com* or another kid search engine such as *www.searchopolis.com* and type several words to define your topic. The more words you use, the more specific your results will be. Say you need to identify the deepest spot in the ocean. For a keyword search, you can type **ocean depths**. But if you type **deepest point in the ocean** as the keywords, the search engine will respond with a shorter list of results. Once again, it's up to you to decide which Web site is most likely to have the answer. Scan the *matching questions,* or, on Searchopolis, the top 10 Web site descriptions, and then make your choice.

Advanced Keyword Tricks

If your *keyword* search *results* don't get you the information you need, you can be even more specific with these advanced tricks. But they don't work on Ask Jeeves for Kids or other kid *search engines.* Test them out on the general search engines listed on page 82.

- **USE PLUS AND MINUS SIGNS.** One trick for power searches is using a simple plus or minus sign. If you want to be sure all results include a word, put a "+" before the word and then click SEARCH. For example, if you want to track down *Web sites* about basketball shoes made of canvas, type **basketball shoes + canvas** and click SEARCH. If you want to make sure the results *don't* include sites about a specific subject, put a "−" before the word that best describes that subject. For example, if you want to find Web sites about boating, but not sailboats, type **boats − sail** and the search engine will leave out sites about sailboats in the results.

- **USE QUOTATION MARKS.** To get still more specific, use quotation marks around your keywords—for example, **"take me out to the ballgame"**—and the search engine will bring back results that include exactly those words in that order, not merely a combination of the words. By using quotation marks, you may be able to bat a thousand on your first try.

👁 **USE SITE-SPECIFIC HELP LINKS.** Just about all general search engines have a HELP link on their main search screen. Some also have an ADVANCED SEARCH link. Try these links for inside tips and tricks on how to be a keyword super-searcher on the particular site you're using.

Eureka!

Searching for a fact on the Internet can be like panning for gold. You have to sift through a lot of information, and there's still no guarantee you'll come up with that precious detail. Like everything else with the Net, the more experience you gain asking questions or searching with *keywords*, the faster you'll become at finding helpful information. Just remember to be patient and persistent. Even the fastest fact finders have to spend some time digging around the World Wide Web in order to strike it rich.

You Be The Judge

Not everything posted on the Net is accurate. As a searcher, you take on

the role of fact judge and jury—also known as making a judgment call. You deliver the verdict on whether or not what you find on the Net is good enough for *your* homework.

But you don't have to make this decision all on your own. Let the Net help you.

Compare the information you find on one *Web site* with another reliable source. Usually you'll get enough *results* from a search to check more than one Web site. Explore a few sites to double-check that the answer you have chosen is correct.

But just how much verifying needs to take place before you can be sure of the facts? Sometimes it's enough to confirm a fact with one other source. For example, if you want to know the birth date of your favorite performer, then confirming one answer you find with another source will do the trick.

If two Web sites have different answers to the same question, you'll need to compare the answer in a book or magazine, or on a third site, to cast the deciding vote. For example, say one site tells you that Mickey Mouse was created in 1955 and another says 1928. Look at a book or magazine to confirm the answer. (By the way, Mickey looks younger than he really is. His official birthday is November 18, 1928, the day the Walt Disney short film *Steamboat Willie*, starring Mickey, was first introduced. Disneyland opened in Southern California in 1955. But don't take my word for it. Verify it by asking Jeeves!)

Remember, anybody can put a Web site up on the Internet. That means some Web sites are a more reliable source for facts than others. See Chapter 3, "Consider the Source," for tips on finding the most trustworthy sites.

TRUTH OR CONSEQUENCES

Use your fact-finding talents to verify which statements below are true and which are wishful thinking, someone's opinion, or flat-out wrong. Write down what you think the answers might be. Then compete with a friend to see who can confirm the answers first. Make a note of the Web site addresses *where you find your answers or print out the pages so you can prove you're right. If you each come up with different answers, then—you guessed it!—it's time to verify your findings with another tie-breaking source.*

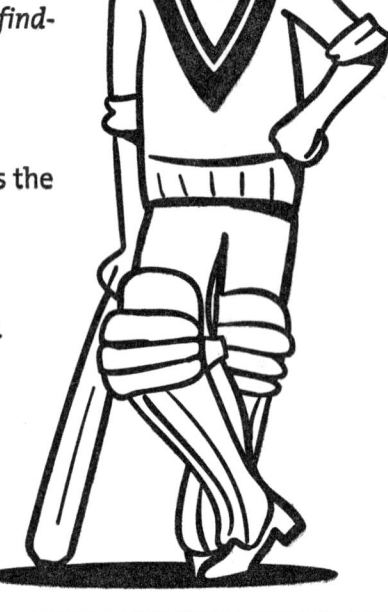

1. The moon has no atmosphere.
2. In the game cricket, the player who jumps the highest wins.
3. Eating carrots improves your eyesight.
4. The gray wolf is no longer an endangered species.
5. A giant spider created the World Wide Web.

Turn to page 22 to check your answers (go ahead, they're reliable!).

 Like a good trial judge, you'll want to keep track of the sources that helped you determine your answer. Turn to Chapter 12, "Collecting Information," to find out how to save a Web site address or a Web page so you can credit the source or refer to it later.

Vanishing Act

Poof! Where does the time go? When you're caught up in the clickable frontier of the Internet, you can lose track of time, and before you know it, it's time to go to bed and there's still no sign of that fact you need.

Clicking is fun, but it's easy to get sidetracked. The key to fact-finding is staying on target like a good detective. Of course, browsing can be a great way to discover and learn, but when time is limited, staying focused works best. Make a list of questions that come up as you do your homework, then let that list guide you when you're online. Before you even log on to the Net, decide how much time you will spend looking for information. Fifteen minutes? An hour? Write it down—then try to stick to it.

Facts Can Be Fascinating

If you want to turn a good report into a great one, be sure to include interesting facts or details. Which statement sounds more interesting to you:

Earthworms live in the ground.

As many as a million earthworms can live in just one acre of farmland.

Facts make everyday subjects come to life. Use the Net to uncover facts that go beyond the run-of-the-mill tidbit, and see your creations—maybe even your grades—improve in a snap.

Puzzling Finds

Whether you search the Net by asking questions or using *keywords*, you will likely get some *results* that are completely unrelated to what you want. Your best bet is just to move along and not dwell on the occasional peculiarity. Just chalk it up to one of the differences between human thought and computer logic.

Truth or Consequences Answers:

1. True. 2. False. 3. True. 4. False. 5. False. (Okay, some things you just know without having to look them up. Lucky you!)

A Case For Gumshoes

Imagine you're a lawyer in a trial about the health benefits of chewing gum. Is chewing gum good for you or is it just fun (or a habit)? You decide which side you're on.

To build your case, you need to find out all you can about gum. Ask Jeeves to help you. Start by asking, **Where can I learn about chewing gum?**

Prepare your argument for the imaginary judge by listing 10 facts you've found about gum that support your position. Do you think you will win the case? See if you can list 10 facts for the other side, too. (Remember, there are at least two sides to every story.)

When you're done, what if the judge congratulates you on being an "excellent gumshoe"? Would that be an insult or a compliment? Ask Jeeves . . . who is somewhat of a gumshoe himself.

CHAPTER 3

Consider the Source

If you need help...

- Evaluating sources
- Finding reliable references
- Creating a bibliography

Start Here

Your little brother is a source of frustration. Fresh ingredients are the source of delicious spaghetti sauce. Reliable Web sites are the source of good grades on your homework. See how powerful—for better or worse—sources can be?

When you approach the Internet for a homework assignment, think of all that electronic information as your library of sources. Lots of words and images compete for your attention. With your mouse in hand and Jeeves at your side, you really are in control, and with that power comes a big challenge.

Meet Your Source

Beyond the words and appealing graphics of a *Web site*, there's a person or team who put that Web site

together. Who are the real people behind the wizard's curtain? Are they who you think they are? For the best results on your assignments, not only do you want to find the best sources, but you want to identify them to give your own work credibility, or trustworthiness.

Use the following strategies to judge which Web sites will give you the most credible information for your homework.

- **EXAMINE FIRST IMPRESSIONS.** When you meet people for the first time, you get instant feelings about them based on how they look and act. You'll get first impressions about Web sites, too. But even online, you'll want to remember not to necessarily judge a book by its cover, so to speak. Sometimes behind the glitz and animation, you'll find a Web site with a questionable purpose. Other times you'll find gems of information buried in dull gray text. Scan the site for evidence of trustworthiness and then trust your reaction.

- **MEET "FACE TO FACE."** Get up close and personal by checking out an ABOUT or BACKGROUND section or another *link* that says it will describe who produced the Web site you're looking at. These links are usually on the *home page*. Why does it matter who created the site? Say you found a nutrition site that promotes the health benefits of glazed jelly donuts. Wise Internet scout that you are, you will want to find the source for this amazing health claim. Reading the ABOUT section, you may discover that the Web site creator is Snappy's Sugar Treats. You might want to take this particular nutritional information with a grain of, uh, salt.

👁 MAP IT OUT. One way to decide if a Web site is legitimate or trustworthy is to review its *site map*. To find the site map, look for a link that says SITE MAP or OVERVIEW. Click the link and examine what you find. Looking over the contents of a Web site will help you get a sense of its purpose. Does the site exist mainly to offer information? To offer something for sale? Do you see a privacy policy? Just like having a casual chat with a new acquaintance, reviewing the site map lets you get more familiar with a site and what it has to offer.

👁 SEEK OUT THE TRIED AND TRUE. In the reference world, reputations count. Some companies have been providing students with homework resources for decades. Most of them have joined the Internet age and have Web sites of their own that you can trust. Look around your classroom or your bookshelves at home for the names and publishers of dictionaries, encyclopedias, almanacs, science magazines, and other reference works. Check to see if they have a Web site address on them, or go to *www.ajkids.com* and ask Jeeves to help you find them on the Internet. Often, if you simply type the name into a typical Web address format, such as *www.encyclopediabritannica.com*, you can find the reference on your own.

Seeing Dots

Another way to get clues about the creator of a *Web site* is to notice the contents of the site's *Web address*, or *URL*. A Web site address usually includes or ends with a "dot" (period) and a three-letter abbreviated word, such as *.com*, which is short for commercial, meaning the site is probably owned by a business or corporation.

Other URL endings include *.net* (network), *.org* (nonprofit organization), *.edu* (educational institution), and *.gov* (government agency). Still, not every .com is a business—some are nonprofits or individuals. Not every .org is a nonprofit—some are businesses.

So how can you use dot clues? As one more piece of information to build your knowledge about a source.

Browser Beware

Seeing is not necessarily believing, especially on the Internet. Anyone can post a site on the Web. And anyone can register that site with *search engines* so it comes up when you do a search for a topic that matches it. But not everyone is an expert or a valid reference. When compiling your sources for an assignment or to back up your facts, you'll want to list sources that you know can be trusted. A personal Web site about someone's experiences visiting the Grand Canyon may be interesting, but if you want to make sure you get your facts right for an assignment on erosion, you'll want to use an official site, such as *www.thecanyon.com/NPS*

Batter Up!

As an Internet searcher, you're really an umpire, calling the plays as you see them, deciding if a *Web site* is "safe" or "out." See if the site hits a

home run or strikes out by asking these questions:

1. What is the motive of the Web site's creators? Are they trying to sell something or persuade me to support their cause?
2. Does the information feel like a fact or an opinion? Do I agree with it? Can the information be confirmed with another source?
3. Do I understand what I'm reading? Is the information written for people my age or at my level in school? How does it compare with what I've studied in class?

The sites you find using Ask Jeeves for Kids at *ajkids.com* are pre*screened* by AJKids editors as reliable sources. This makes your job as an umpire a lot easier!

Bibliographies

When creating a report or project, you will often be asked by your teacher to make a bibliography. The word bibliography once referred to a list of books—books consulted by an author or books on a particular topic. But times—and technologies—have changed. Today a bibliography includes not only books but movies, CDs, and, of course, Internet sources. When your teacher asks for a bibliography, she or he probably wants information on *all* the sources you used for a project. You'll need to include such details as the title of the source, the author, and the date each work was produced.

The individual listings in a bibliography will contain different information, depending on the form of the original source. For example, a book listing will show information that is different from the credit for a *Web site* listing. For one thing, Web sites change frequently, so it's important to note the date you found your information. Here's one way to credit an online source (an imaginary magazine article):

FORMAT:

Author's last name, author's first name. "Article Title." *Magazine Title*. Date or period posted on the Web: number of paragraphs. Place you found it. Available: *Web site address*. Accessed: date you saw it.

EXAMPLE:

Palluza, Hula. "Dancing Makes You Happy." *Hip-Hip Hooray Magazine*. May 2004: 7 pars. Online. Available: *www.shakealeg555.com*. Accessed: May 5, 2004.

For more tips on citing Internet sources, including e-mail sources, visit *www.uvm.edu/~ncrane/estyles/mla.html* or ask Jeeves at *ajkids.com*, **How do I cite Internet sources?**

Your teacher might assign you a specific format to follow for your bibliography. For details and examples of a variety of bibliography formats, visit the Modern Language Association at *www.mla.org/style/style_index.htm*. Or ask Jeeves, **How do I create a bibliography?**

Expiration Dates

One of the benefits of doing research on the Net is that you have access to the very latest information and discoveries. Most credible or dependable *Web sites* are updated frequently. Look over a *home page* to see if it says when it was last updated. If a Web site on Prince William hasn't been updated for a year, then you know it contains old news.

Fact vs. Opinion

Newspapers, magazines, TV, Web sites, even books about Web sites—all mix fact with opinion. Facts are indisputable, or certain, while opinions can be as different as the people who offer them.

Which of the following statements are facts and which are opinions? (See page 32 for the answers.)

1. Montreal is the most beautiful city in Canada.
2. Mark McGuire hit 70 home runs in the 1999 baseball season.
3. *The Color Purple* by Alice Walker is an excellent book for understanding the American South.
4. Grace Murray Hopper invented the first modern computer language.
5. A glass of water can be half empty and half full at the same time.

HINT: When you're not sure if a statement is a fact or an opinion, try putting it into this sentence: "It is my opinion that [statement]." If it's a fact, that sentence is going to sound pretty silly!

Deliveries by Jeeves

When you ask Jeeves to help you track down Web sites for your homework, you'll notice that a lot of funny-looking symbols and numbers show up in the *Web site address*, or *URL*, bar. It gives you a good idea of the great lengths your butler pal will go to find what you need. But this information will look pretty strange in your bibliography. You'll want to go a step further to make finding the site easier for your teacher.

To get the Web site's address, simply click the words NO FRAMES in the upper left corner of the screen. The top part of the page that says ASK JEEVES FOR KIDS will disappear, and the URL on your *browser* will change. Now you have the official address for this Web page. Jot it down for your bibliography. Better yet, use your copy and paste tools (see page 84) to copy the string of letters and numbers into a word-processing document. That way you can avoid typing mistakes!

Where Credit's Due

What's the big deal about citing your homework sources? Crediting someone for information that you use or quote directly is important for three reasons:

1. It pays respect to the person whose hard work helped you.
2. It makes your homework credible—that is, trustworthy. Your readers (for example, your teachers!) will know which ideas are yours and which ideas are from

someone else. After all, you want to get credit for your original thoughts.

3. It covers you with the law. It's illegal to publish someone else's work without giving him or her credit.

To learn more about why crediting your sources is a good idea, see "Copy Rights." PAGE 85

Fact vs. Opinion Answers

1. Opinion: Words like "beautiful" or "friendly" are a good sign that a statement is an opinion.
2. Fact: In 1999, McGuire broke the record for home runs in a single season.
3. Opinion: *The Color Purple* is about the American South, and although many people think it is a good book, that's still a matter of opinion.
4. Fact: Grace Murray Hopper, a mathematician and rear admiral in the U.S. Navy, was a member of the team that created the first programmable digital computer in the 1940s.
5. Fact: Some people see it one way; some people see it the other way. The fact is, both are true.

Homonymous

Site. Cite. Sight. With all the different sightings going on in the name of your homework, you might start seeing things after a while. Don't be confused by words that sound the same, or homonyms. A homonym plays tricks on the ears, but the eyes know better.

Site means a location, as in a campsite or Web site. *Cite* means to recognize, quote, or mention, as in cite a reference. *Sight* means the powers of your eyes to make sense of all these same-sounding words—and the wild variety of things you find on the Net—as well as a place to visit when you go sightseeing.

Be on the lookout! Ask Jeeves, **Where can I find a list of homonyms?** and get clear on some other words you have to see to believe.

CHAPTER 4
Get the Picture

If you need help...

- Writing a report, poem, or journal
- Completing a project
- Illustrating your work

Start Here

Sometimes the only thing between you and a blank piece of paper or a blinking cursor on a computer screen is knowing how to put one little word in front of the other. You just need to see how it's done, then you'll be on your way! When you feel panic set in because you don't have a clue about starting your homework... or you've started but now you're facing writer's block... or you're just about done but not sure how to wrap the whole thing up, you need inspiration in the form of examples and ideas.

Or maybe what's stumping you is that you have to illustrate your work. Teachers often ask for illustrations as part of science projects or writing assignments. You may have to choose photos, create drawings, or make diagrams. Illustrations help your projects come to life—and can even get you a better grade.

Write On!

For advice on writing, start by going to *www.ajkids.com* and asking Jeeves, **How do I write a book report?** or **Where can I get advice on writing a poem?** Ask a question that directly applies to your homework assignment. Or explore *www.writesite.org* to see how the Web might support your work.

Often you'll find sites that offer homework support for a broad range of ages. Don't get hung up if you don't understand what a site is talking about or if it seems too young for you. You certainly don't need the frustration! Just COB (Click On By)!

Project: Completion

Excuse me for stating the obvious, but getting started on a project is the first major step to finishing it. Finding ideas on the Internet will get your own creative juices flowing. Before you know it, you'll be pulling it all together. Go to Jeeves and ask, **What are some ideas for science projects?** Or ask about a specific project, for example **How do I make a family tree?**

For a *keyword* search using a kid *search engine* such as *www.lycoszone.com*, try simply typing **science projects** and you'll find more than a dozen sites with examples and ideas—*www.spartechsoftware.com/reeko* and *http://nyelabs.kcts.org*, for example.

Make sure you consider the differences between an experiment and a project. An *experiment* is an activity that tests an idea or confirms a fact. For instance, touching objects with a magnet helps confirm whether or not an object contains iron. A *project* is a planned activity usually carried out over time. Collecting leaves from different trees in your neighborhood, putting them in a booklet you make, and labeling them would be a project.

It's a good idea to get your teacher's approval for a long-term project topic before you start, just to know you're on the right track.

Another way to get examples and ideas for an assignment is to turn to people with a little more experience than you. See Chapter 5, "Ask an Expert."

Picture Perfect

If you think about your favorite Web sites, books, or magazines, one of the things you probably like most is the way they look. The layout, colors, photographs, art—and the words—are designed in a way that's pleasing to you.

Usually, images help explain the subject, too. It's one thing to read about a wombat, but it's another thing to see a picture of one of the furry creatures. You get a better idea of what the animal is like in an instant. By illustrating your work, you improve your communication with the reader... and the grader!

Whether your assignment is electronic or on paper, you can find lots of ideas for creating the right look:

- **REVIEW YOUR PEERS' WORK.** See how some kids' authors illustrate their work at *www.yahooligans.com/School_Bell/Language_Arts/Illustrators*

- **COLLECT ONLINE CLIP ART.** You can print *clip art* or copy and paste it into the software program you are using. Ask Jeeves, **Where can I find free clip art?** Or use another search engine to do a *keyword* search for **free clip art**. The Internet is loaded with free art. Remember, the real keyword here is *free*!

> **Less Is More**
>
> If you take the time to find lots of interesting ways to illustrate or present your project, you might be tempted to use everything on hand. In most cases, though, more isn't better. Pick and choose the best ideas and examples. If you are using clip art, choose the pictures that will improve, or enhance, what your work communicates to readers. Too much of a good thing can be distracting.

👁 **MAKE IT YOURS.** Print the art you find and use other tools, like markers and crayons, to make your presentation more original. If you're working on a computer with a color printer, you can even use a simple graphics program to add colored boxes and text. Color is a great way to make something more interesting.

The Long and Short of It

How long should an essay or report be? Often your teacher will give you guidelines. Other times she or he will simply offer the dreaded suggestion that you make your project as long as it "needs to be." Ask yourself these questions so you can judge the long and short of it for yourself.

👁 Do I clearly state my main idea or ideas?

- 👁 Have I repeated ideas or facts more than necessary?
- 👁 Can I state three or more facts about my main topic?
- 👁 Can I add more details to describe my subject?
- 👁 Do I give supporting evidence or cite outside sources for my statements?
- 👁 Is the information organized so a reader can understand it?
- 👁 Have I noted opposing views and given proof of why I think I'm right?
- 👁 What will readers take away from my work? Have I answered questions they might have?

Use your answers to beef up or cut down a report as needed. Have a parent or friend read your work before you turn it in to see how they react.

Keep on Scrolling

Web pages are bordered by *scroll bars*, which help you move around the site. If you don't scroll around, you might be missing something good. Depending on the size of your computer screen, details can be tucked out of view. To make sure you see all that a Web page has to offer, be sure to scroll up and down and to the left and right. When you've had enough, move on to another site.

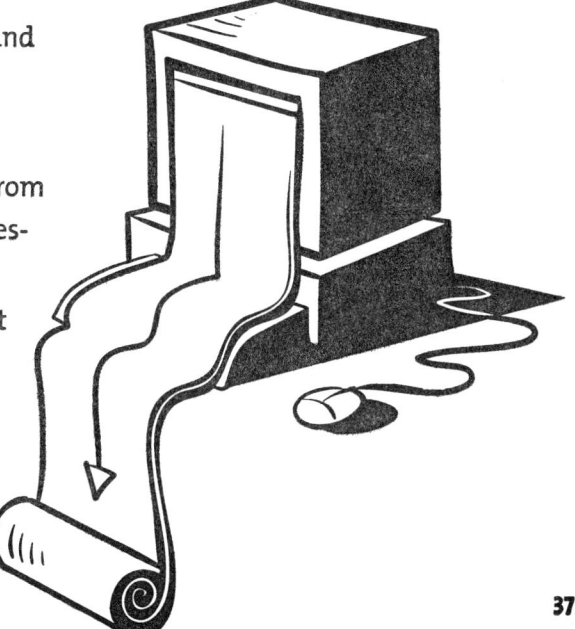

For Your Eyes Only

Sometimes you don't even know what you think until you write it down. Have you ever tried keeping a written record of your thoughts? Keeping a personal journal or diary about your experiences, friendships, and beliefs can be one of the treasures of your lifetime. You can chronicle your secrets, track your ups and downs, work out problems, and sort through life's events.

The best part about keeping a personal journal is that you never have a deadline. You decide when you're in the mood to write and when you're not. If you don't have one already, try starting your own journal. Use these ideas to help you get writing:

- If you could sum up your day in 10 words or less, what would they be?
- What did you do after school?
- Right now, you wish you could go to _____.
- What really bugged you today or made you happy?
- Who are your best friends?
- What are your favorite activities?

Feel free to doodle in the margins, paste in pictures, or write a poem. Add anything that gives you a sense of who you really are! For more ideas, ask Jeeves, **Where can I get advice on keeping a journal?**

CHAPTER 5

Ask an Expert

If you need help...

- Getting online homework help
- Answering a tricky question
- Understanding a concept

Start Here

Does the Web site you're turning to for help raise more questions than it answers? For all the information the World Wide Web offers, sometimes nothing replaces getting answers directly from a human being. Luckily for you, many teachers, librarians, and other experts help students online, often as volunteers.

Still, it isn't always possible to get immediate, person-to-person help on the Internet at any time of the day or night.

Some sites claim to be *question-and-answer (Q&A)* sites—places where you can submit a question and an expert will send you the answer. But some of these sites answer only one question a month. Others say they will answer any question, but it may take two days to two weeks for them to get back to you—long after your assignment is due. Operators are not standing by.

That said, seeking a response from a real live person can be a rewarding experience in your efforts to learn on the Internet. Just ask Jeeves to arrange an introduction for you!

First, What's an Expert?

An expert is a person who thoroughly knows a subject or has mastered a skill, often through firsthand experience. You might say you're a math expert because you know how to add and subtract and you do it every day. Indeed, you are an expert in addition and subtraction! But "math expert" might be a stretch.

A classmate may claim to be a lion expert because she went to the zoo and saw one. Still, unless she has researched lions, written about them, or observed how they live in the wild, she won't be a very reliable resource for you.

By now you probably get the picture. Who qualifies to be an expert and who doesn't qualify can often be a matter of opinion. Whenever you decide that you need to seek assistance from an expert online, you will also want to seek information about that expert. Check out the ABOUT or BACKGROUND section of the expert's Web site. If you can't learn more about the expert, move on to your next choice.

Ask Jeeves to Find an Expert

To get the latest list of Web sites offering expert assistance, go to *www.ajkids.com* and ask Jeeves, **Where can I find an expert to answer my question?** Another way to get support for a specific subject is to ask Jeeves, **Where can I ask a math question?** or **Where can I ask a science question?** Jeeves will set you up with many sites that can give you a response.

Read the Fine Print

The temptation to click and flit around online is as mighty as the urge to slurp down a chocolate milkshake. To get what you need on the Internet, though, sometimes you have to read directions and swallow information slowly. Taking the time to follow the instructions on a Q&A site will save you time—and perhaps a virtual stomachache or "ice cream headache"—in the long run.

Instant Answers

Most *Web sites* offering expert assistance also keep an *archive*, or collection, of all previous questions and answers or at least the most *frequently asked questions (FAQs)*. If you need an answer right away, or you're not sure exactly what you need, review a site's archive or FAQs for assistance. Often archives are organized by subject to make a search easier and quicker. In fact, you can save time by always checking the archive or FAQs before even submitting a question.

You'll find sites that have rules like these:

- 👁 Some sites will answer a question only once. If your question is answered in their *archive*, they will not respond to your e-mail, and you'll be left waiting.

- 👁 Other online experts will choose only one question from all the questions they receive in a time period (such as a day or a week) and answer it only on a message board, requiring you to visit frequently to see if your question is answered.

- 👁 Some sites answer directly by e-mail, but they require a certain time frame to respond, usually at least two days, maybe longer.

Build Your Own Support System

Though they may not be as convenient as having your own personal "answering service," online experts are eager to help you. Ask Jeeves, **Where can I find homework help?** or enter the *keywords* **homework help** and you'll get *results* that are chock-full of options.

Use the homework-help sites you find to build your own personalized support network. Get familiar with these resources *before* you need them. Which sites explain subjects or define terms? Which sites discuss every language-arts topic ever imagined? Note the sites you like most with your *browser's bookmark* or *favorites* tool. Now you have places to turn to in a crisis.

Visit the Web sites listed below to start your own homework support system. But remember: Web sites change frequently. If one of these sites doesn't work anymore, go back and ask Jeeves for more ideas!

- When you can't visit your school library, the Internet Public Library is the next best thing. It's loaded with references and other materials. Visit the kid site at *www.ipl.org/youth/*

- Do you need to know how televisions or toilets work? If you have a science project or an engineering question, go to *www.howstuffworks.com*

- Hook up with experts at the Center for Improved Engineering and Science Education at *http://njnie.dl.stevens-tech.edu/askanexpert.html*

- Still stumped by that math challenge? This doctor makes house calls! Doctor Math answers questions and lists previous Q&As for your reference at *http://forum.swarthmore.edu/dr.math*

- Through the American Library Association, volunteer media specialists will answer questions in two days at KidsConnect, *www.ala.org/ICONN/AskKC.html*

- You can ask the librarians at The Toronto Public Library to look up dates, names, spellings, addresses, facts, definitions, book titles, and URLs. Drop them an e-mail at *www.tpl.toronto.on.ca/TRL/centres/answer/form/epl.html*

- The Department of Geology and Geophysics at the University of Hawaii offers an Ask-an-Earth-Scientist service and a handy archive of previously asked questions. Give it a try at *www.soest.hawaii.edu/GG/ASK/askanerd.html*

- Meet over 150 great Canadian scientists and ask them questions at *www.science.ca/ask/*

T-Ref

If you happen to find a thesaurus in your homework-help escapades, don't run the other way. Although its name might sound like a type of long-gone dinosaur, the mighty thesaurus can be one of the most important references you'll ever have.

A thesaurus is like a dictionary, but rather than defining what a word means, it provides a list of other words that mean the same thing, or synonyms. A thesaurus will usually offer antonyms, or words that mean the opposite, as well.

Everyone needs help thinking of a new or different word now and then. Suppose you've used the word "perfect" four times in one paragraph—a bit much. If you look up "perfect" in a thesaurus, you'll find a list of other words you can use, such as "excellent," "ideal," and "pure." Some thesauruses even tell you how to use words by showing them in a sentence.

Use a thesaurus to fill in the blanks below and finish a description about you!

1. Go to the Merriam-Webster Web site at *www.m-w.com/thesaurus.htm*

2. Do a search for these words:

    intrepid
    deft
    magnanimous

3. Choose the synonym you like best for each one.

4. Write them in the blanks:

    I am _____, _____, and _____!

Since there's more than one synonym for each word, your answer can be as individual as you are.

CHAPTER 6
Use the News

If you need help...

- Tracking a current event
- Gathering the latest information
- Reporting your story

Start Here

It's a dog's life, hounding down news on the World Wide Web. Where can you get current events for your homework projects without going through a major search-and-rescue operation? Let a well-bred resource like Jeeves sniff around the Internet for you. You might even want to have news delivered to you daily—retrieved and brought to your footstool in the form of a personal *Web site* update. You play the responsible master and teach the Internet to follow your commands.

Being "in the know" means you're up-to-date on the events in the world and community around you. Someone who's "out of touch" hasn't heard about the latest major news events. You're a kid, so you're not expected to know everything, thank goodness. Yet being in the know, even a little bit, can help you in big ways, at school and in life.

Keeping Current

Reading about current events does more than deliver extra credit in school. Jeeves would be the first to agree that knowing what's going on in your world offers many benefits:

- The latest news can give you fresh ideas for report topics and other assignments.

- News can help you plan ahead. A gasoline shortage, labor strike, or major storm—can all change your plans for the next day, overnight.

- News can inspire you to live a healthier life, get involved in your community, and be sympathetic to the problems of others.

Still, for all the good news about knowing the news, you have to be cautious:

- Dramatic headlines, intended to cause excitement and hook readers, can be misleading.

- Not everything you read is true—reporters make mistakes, just like everyone else.

- A lot of the news is bad news and can be depressing or give you a dark view of the world.

As with everything you do on the Internet, be an active participant in your news site searches. Pick and choose your resources with care and read them with a sharp eye.

Extra! Extra! Read All About It!

On the Net, you can read about current events on *Web sites* made just for kids—some sites have news especially of interest to kids, and some even have news reported by kids. Go to *www.ajkids.com* and ask Jeeves, **Where can I find newspaper Web sites for kids?** or **Where can I find magazine sites for kids?**

Scout out these sites, too:

> Time for Kids at *www.timeforkids.com*
>
> Scholastic News Zone at *http://teacher.scholastic.com/newszone/index.asp*
>
> Vocal Point at *http://bvsd.k12.co.us/cent/Newspaper*
>
> KIDS Report at *http://kids.library.wisc.edu*

Where in the World?

Most big-city newspapers have online editions. That means you can read news that has happened in just about any city in North America or even the world if you need to or want to.

Suppose you live in Vancouver, Canada, and you're writing a report on the effects of a big fire in the state of New Mexico. Your local newspaper may write an article about the fire, but a paper in Santa Fe or Albuquerque will naturally cover it in more detail. Wouldn't it be impressive if you quoted the local fire department officers in your report? Or maybe your class is following the election of a new Parliament of England. You can get the very latest details on the issues at the Web site for the *London Times*: *www.the-times.co.uk*

To find newspapers with local angles, ask Jeeves, **Where can I find newspapers online?**

Your Personal Page

Many *browsers* and general *search engines* let you create a *personal page*, or start-up page, when you visit their *Web sites*. For example, at Ask Jeeves at *www.ask.com* (the adult version of Ask Jeeves for Kids), there is such a service, called Personal Jeeves. You can tailor your page to your personal interests by following a few simple editing instructions. For example, you can pick what news subjects and weather reports you want to see, and the site will automatically update your page when you log on.

NOTE: This is an activity to do with a parent or other adult. Web sites require that you register your name and a password when you get a personal page. Anytime you register at a Web site, you want to have an adult assist you, because the site may ask for personal information during the registration process. An adult can help you choose what information to provide and what to keep private.

 For more information on protecting your privacy on the Internet, see "Private Practices." (PAGE 90)

Fresh Daily

What makes news news? With current events, timing is everything. News is considered news when it's an event that just happened. Otherwise, old news is history, really.

With the Internet, news delivery has taken on a whole new meaning. Rather than waiting for the morning edition of your local paper to land at your door, you can often read about the latest news events the night before, online—especially if the matter in question took place in an earlier time

THE FIVE W'S

You've probably recited the Five W's in school: who, what, when, where, and why ("how" is often thrown in, too). The Five W's make up the Journalism Golden Rule. Every news story should answer these questions in the first few sentences.

Now it's your turn to evaluate whether or not online journalists follow this rule:

1. Go to a newspaper site and pick an interesting story. Look for the Five W's. Are any left out? Do they appear in the very beginning of the story?
2. You be the editor. How would you make the story better?
3. Sharpen your journalistic instincts. Write a story about the last time you and your friends got together for a special event, such as a birthday. Or report on an event you *wish* would happen. Try using the five W's and leading off with an "inverted pyramid" (see below).

zone. If you're working on a current event report due the next day or you want to see whether your favorite sports team won a game and you can't wait until the nightly news on TV, visit a news *Web site* to get the scoop.

Upside-Down Pyramids

The upside-down, or *inverted*, pyramid is a technique many journalists use to grab readers. A lot of information—especially the most interesting stuff—is packed in the first few sentences, then the rest of the story fleshes out the details. The inverted pyramid style of writing not only gets your attention, it also allows you to read only the headline and first paragraph and still get the main points in a story if you're tight on time—a good strategy for scanning stories on the Net.

This story by Lucy Lehrer in Scholastic's News Zone (at *http://teacher.scholastic.com/newszone/index.asp*) uses the inverted pyramid to draw you into a story about a "deep" subject:

Cracks on the Ocean Floor
By Lucy Lehrer

Large cracks on the Atlantic Ocean floor could be an early warning sign of landslides and tidal waves, scientists reported today.

The cracks were found along a 25-mile section of the Atlantic Ocean off the coasts of Virginia and North Carolina. Scientists announced the discovery of the cracks in this month's issue of the scientific journal *Geology*. **Geology** is the study of Earth's layers of soil and rock.

Scientists say the cracks could cause a **tsunami** (tsoo-NAH-mee), or a tidal wave, that could send 18-foot waves toward the East Coast of the U.S. Tsunamis are usually caused by earthquakes, but landslides on the ocean floor can also trigger the enormous waves.

Scientists will continue to gather more information about the cracks. They will install monitoring devices on the bottom of the ocean to keep track of whether or not the cracks are moving.

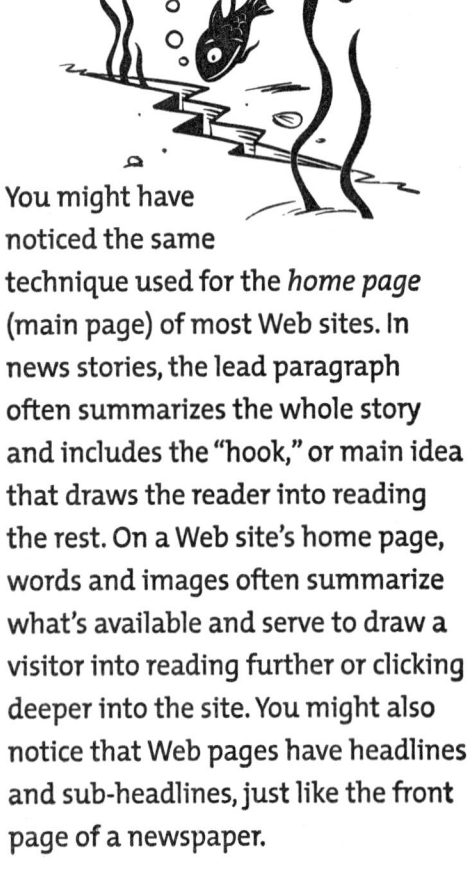

You might have noticed the same technique used for the *home page* (main page) of most Web sites. In news stories, the lead paragraph often summarizes the whole story and includes the "hook," or main idea that draws the reader into reading the rest. On a Web site's home page, words and images often summarize what's available and serve to draw a visitor into reading further or clicking deeper into the site. You might also notice that Web pages have headlines and sub-headlines, just like the front page of a newspaper.

 If you're a journalist at heart and love to report and interpret the news happening around you, you can connect with news Web sites made by and for kids. See Chapter 7, "Make Contact," for ideas.

PART TWO

Jeeves, I Need Life Help!

Ah, the ups and downs of life. So many fun things to do, interests to explore, problems to solve. In many ways, the most unlikely place a person would look to fulfill their hopes and dreams would be a machine plugged into the wall.

But while it shouldn't be the only place you look for support and answers to life's questions, tracking down valuable resources on the World Wide Web can be one of your tactics for riding out roller-coaster times and adding to good times.

This section helps you get connected, once you've gotten wired. With Internet access, you can hook up with clubs, other kids, experts, and useful guides. Jeeves leads you to sites that offer guidance, ideas, and solutions. Along the way, you can get creative and show your colors or share your ideas with others.

On the Net you'll find you're not alone, but still one of a kind!

CHAPTER 7

Make Contact

If you need help...

- Connecting with friends
- Meeting new people
- Joining online discussions

Start Here

It's one thing to be wired—it's another thing to be connected.

Being wired without being connected is like getting all dressed up with no place to go. You have a computer, an *Internet service provider,* and an e-mail address. So now it's time to hook up with other kids on the Internet. How do you get started? Where do you fit in? How do you connect?

You might have a few friends you swap e-mails with already. But there are plenty of other people you can connect with, in places all around the world. What about the kids in other countries with interests like yours? Without a face-to-face meeting, making friends on the Internet can at first seem as hard as, if not harder than, making friends in real life. Allow Jeeves to introduce you.

The more connections and good relationships you have in life, the better you feel and the better you can weather any kind of storm. Besides, it's just plain fun.

How Do You Do

There are different levels of interaction with people on the Internet. Choose the level that suits you.

LIVE CHATS. Picture yourself sitting at a lunchroom table talking with your friends about the movie you saw over the weekend and getting silly with your French fries, and you can imagine a *live chat*. Several Web sites host chats for kids. Ask Jeeves at *www.ajkids.com*, **Where can I find online chats for kids?** You might even find a live chat with the movie star in the blockbuster you saw over the weekend. Explore the sites and their rules. Keep in mind that you will need your parent's or guardian's permission to *register*, or sign up.

DISCUSSION BOARDS. A *discussion board*, or message board, is a place where you can share your ideas and read what others have to say. Most boards are set up to create an ongoing exchange on a particular topic or area of interest. For example, you might find a board where you can share your opinion on topics like school uniforms or violence in the media or where you can post stories about your pet or about the fun things you did at camp. Many Web sites for kids have discussion boards. Ask Jeeves, **Where can I find message boards?** As with online chats, you will be required to *register* for most discussion boards.

INSTANT MESSAGING. Some *Internet service providers (ISPs)*, such as America Online, offer *instant messaging* that lets you send and receive message alerts while you are online. Instant messages are handy when you and the person you're writing to are online at the same time. There's no sense in waiting for an e-mail to get to you. An instant message pops up on your computer screen right after someone sends it, and then you can respond. Check the *home page* of your ISP to find instructions for setting up instant messaging with your friends and e-pals.

Another way to hook up with others on the Internet is to join an online club that centers on one of your interests. See Chapter 8, "Take a Break," for more tips.
PAGE 60

To Whom It May Concern

If you ever want to make a point, put it in writing. Whether you're sending sentiments of love, criticism, sympathy, or good news, the written word can carry more weight than a spoken message. When you write an important e-mail, use the same instincts you use for writing a letter. You want to be clear and use accurate grammar and spelling. Put your best foot forward.

Chit Chat Challenge

When you join a *live chat*—the speediest of all written messages—you can be more casual than when writing a regular e-mail, but there are still things you can do to make a good impression.

Try these tips:

- 👁 **THINK ABOUT OTHERS.** The best chat experiences involve give and take. What can you contribute to a discussion? How can you respond to what someone just wrote?

- 👁 **STAY ON THE TOPIC.** If you're in a chat room where the topic is soccer, you'll do everyone a favor if you limit yourself to talking about soccer and don't go off on a story about your family trip to an amusement park. If you get bored, go to another chat room where the topic is more interesting to you.

- 👁 **FOLLOW SITE RULES.** Good manners still count, even on the World Wide Web. Most chats for kids are monitored by adults. You will be booted from a chat room if you do not follow a site's rules. Look them over before you start. They exist so others don't take away from your fun.

Learn more about getting alone with others online in Chapter 13, "Follow the Peas and Cues (or Netiquette)."

PAGE 87

Greetings, Anyone?

Online greeting cards can be a fun and creative way to send a note to someone you're thinking about. One of the *Web sites* that allow you to do this is *www.bluemountain.com*, which offers cards for just about every occasion. Ask Jeeves, **Where can I find online greeting cards?** You'll find links to other greeting card sites for your age group or to suit a particular purpose. Some sites give you the option to make your own card using scanned photos. Remember, if you're ever asked to *register* at a Web site, get your parents involved so they can help you make decisions about what information to give out.

e-Pals for Life

One of the best things about the Internet is your freedom to travel among the countries of the world without having to worry about a passport or visa for admission—or the cash to pay for a trip.

Just as people have pen pals in other countries—friends they get to know by exchanging letters—you can find and get to know an "e-pal" through e-mail. A few *Web sites* will match you with a kid in another country so you can share stories about your life and interests. Who knows? You might become lifelong friends!

Go to *www.ipfs.org* or ask Jeeves, **Where can I connect with an online pen pal?**

Family Ties

Some people complain that computers and the Internet make people isolated, but it all depends on the user. Computers are wonderful tools for keeping in contact with family members you don't see regularly, like a cousin who is your age or your favorite uncle or aunt.

Reach out online. Once you start using e-mail, you'll find a number of your relatives doing the same—using e-mail to stay in touch. Since most *Internet service* providers (ISPs) charge a flat fee for unlimited hours, you can take advantage of Internet access to strengthen family ties without paying another cent. Contact relatives to discuss family news, plan visits, and, if you have access to a scanner or digital camera, send them recent pictures.

👁 **CREATE A FAMILY WEB PAGE.** One way to stay in touch with family members is to create a Web page through a free service such as *www.myfamily.com*. Most ISPs offer space for a free Web page as well. You can share photos and information about upcoming events and activities.

NOTE: Sites offering free Web pages require you to *register*. Have a parent register with you, then make your page a family affair and get a parent or sibling to create it with you.

👁 **CLIMB YOUR FAMILY TREE.** You can get more familiar with your family's roots at *www.ancestry.com* or *www.familyhistory.com*. If you're interested, you can even start mapping out your family tree. For more resources, ask Jeeves, **How do I trace my family tree?**

CHAPTER 8

Take a Break

If you need help...

- Exploring an interest
- Developing a hobby
- Trading experiences with others

Start Here

You might not realize it, but at this very moment you have at least one hobby lurking around in the nooks and crannies of your brain. We all have a natural-born desire to collect, create, explore, talk about, read about, and otherwise participate in something we find interesting. "So," you may be wondering, "what's my hobby?"

Some kids collect cards, souvenirs, rocks, stuffed animals, or other favorite things. Others are into jewelry-making, models, painting, or any number of crafts. Your hobby can be a sport you play or an activity you like to do, such as listening to music or going to the movies. Think about your own interests, then explore them further online. Ask Jeeves at *www.ajkids.com* a simple question, like **Where can I learn about music online?**

If you are already involved in a particular hobby, sport, or interest, you might want specific information about it. Whatever your situation is, you can use the Internet as a tool to explore and share your hobbies and interests. The strategies in this chapter can make your Internet experience a more meaningful one.

For Kids Only

To explore an interest on the Internet, you want to find sites designed for you. Sites created especially for kids give you an advantage. They're not for babies. Kid sites are for people like you who share similar interests and study the same things in school.

Kid sites offer you more than adult sites can. Say your hobby is inventing funny gadgets. You'll find much more support for your ideas at the kid site of the United States Patent and Trademarks Office than you will at the agency's site for adults. See for yourself at *www.uspto.gov*. Click the Kids' Pages *link* to judge the difference. Whenever you ask Jeeves a question or conduct a search about your hobby on the Internet, try adding the word "kid" or "kids" to get information tailored for you. You could ask Jeeves, **Where can I learn about the kids' activity or hobby _____?** Fill in the blank with your hobby and see what comes up.

Join the Club

The best way to trade experiences or stories about your hobby is to join a club with kids who have the same interest. Joining an online community also helps you increase your skills or knowledge over time, through online *chats* and other exchanges. Chances are that an Internet-based club already exists for your hobby, and you'll be able to connect with kids all over North America and maybe the world.

Find out about clubs by asking Jeeves a question like **Where can I find a comic book collector's club?** and then explore the *results*. To see a few kid clubs online, go to *www.peak.org/~bonwritr/links.htm*. Some kids' clubs may require a fee to join.

If you don't find a club that suits your needs, get together with some of your friends and start your own club. Ask Jeeves, **How do I start my own club?** Eventually you can try creating a *home page* for your club using your *Internet service provider (ISP)* account. Most ISPs offer one personal home page per account—check the home page of yours for details.

Commercial Break

Most *Web sites* offering a free service—such as a *personal Web page*, games, or Internet *searches*—support their businesses through advertising. They sell space on their site to other businesses that want to reach potential customers with messages about products. Some Web sites that sell products also offer useful information about your hobby or interest.

Avoid confusion when you're exploring a site. Notice which *icons* or *links* on a site are regular features and which are links for ads or sales. Often a Web page will mark the ad and shopping links with clear labels.

NOTE: You'll always need your parent's or guardian's permission—and credit card—to shop online.

Stargazing

If you have a favorite music group, TV show, actor, or movie, you'll find plenty of information on the Internet to fuel your interest. Just about every hot star or show gets in on the Net act these days. You can *register* at the *Web sites* of your favorites to get e-mails about upcoming events and tour dates, to ask stars or producers questions, to join fan clubs, and even to order CDs, videos, and posters if your parents agree to cover the costs.

You can get TV schedules for Nick at Nite, TV Land, and other favorite channels or go behind the scenes of a blockbuster movie. Just ask Jeeves to help you with a question like **Where can I find information on 'N Sync?**

You also can try *keywords* with a conventional *search engine* such as www.yahooligans.com to catch your stars online.

If your hobby is looking at *real* stars, ask Jeeves, **Where can I see pictures of outer space?** You'll see some of our most distant galaxy neighbors up close and personal.

Link-o-Rama

In your Internet travels, almost every site you come across will offer you a list of recommended *links* to other related sites. Such lists are usually worth a look. You can discover sites that you haven't found in your own *searches*. A collection of pre-screened links saves you searching time in the long run. Just make sure the site giving the recommendations is a site that you trust. Then browse their recommendations and mark the ones you want to come back to.

The Scoop on Downloads

If you want to listen to music online or watch videos and animations, your computer will need the latest *software*, or *plug-ins*. Since technology is always changing, plug-ins are constantly being improved and updated. The good news is that sites requiring particular software programs usually offer a convenient *link* to *download* the latest programs for free.

Say you're visiting a Web site and you click an *icon* to hear a new song. If your computer needs certain software to play it, the site will ask if you want to download the software. But before you click OK, know that downloads take time. Depending on the speed of your Internet connection, downloads can take anywhere from 10 minutes to more than an hour. Most of the plug-ins you'll need should require less than an hour to download.

NOTE: Before you download any software from the Internet, check with your parents to make sure the software will work on your computer and that your computer has enough hard-drive storage available.

CHAPTER 9
Get Creative

If you need help...

- ☞ Developing creative skills
- ☞ Sharing your creations
- ☞ Getting useful feedback

Start Here

*This is my letter to the world,
That never wrote to me;
The simple news that Nature told,
With tender majesty.*

*Her message is committed
To hands I cannot see;
For love of her, sweet countrymen,
Judge tenderly of me!*

—Emily Dickinson

The words of American poet Emily Dickinson could very well echo how you feel about sharing your work with others. When you share your writings, your drawings, or any creative expression with other people, you open yourself to their criticism or their praise. Either way, a person's reaction to your work can depress you or encourage you. You want them to treat you tenderly.

Even with the risk of disapproval, though, most artists and writers feel the need to share their work with others. Having someone else see and maybe appreciate your creation makes you feel like part of something bigger.

The World Wide Web can make you feel that way, too. If you like to draw or write, you will find online *communities* to acknowledge and support your work. Just like the real-world guidance of teachers and mentors, the Net can be a useful resource for developing your talents.

Happy Medium

In the art world, the term *medium* is singular for *media*, or the mode that you use to express your talents. If you enjoy visual arts, these are just a few of the forms you can try out:

- computer graphics
- charcoal or pen-and-ink drawing
- pastels
- watercolors
- photography
- pottery
- embroidery
- sculpture
- carving

Expressions in writing can take many forms as well:

poetry

news and feature stories

short stories

essays

movie or theater reviews

plays or screenplays

Ask Jeeves questions at *www.ajkids.com* to find out more about a medium that appeals to you. You can ask, **Where can I learn to draw with pastels?** or **How do I write a play?** or **What's a good photography site for kids?**

Often the medium or format you use reflects what you want to say. For instance, if you want to document a news event, you could write a feature article. If you want to get across how you feel about something, you might want to write a poem. In other words, the medium becomes part of the message. Think about how your message and different media could work together. Don't forget to consider *multimedia* formats, too, like video or animation combined with sound.

Blank Page

Every artist starts with a blank page, computer screen, canvas, drawing pad, roll of film, or mound of clay. Sometimes they—or you—get stuck. No matter how hard you stare at the tools of your trade, the ideas simply won't come. Writer's or artist's block has struck again! At times like these, you can turn to the Internet for ideas and inspiration.

One way to stir your imagination is to see what others have done. For example, ask Jeeves, **Where can I find an online gallery where kids show their art?** or **Where can I read other kids' work?** Viewing other kids' creations may give you thoughts about how to start or shape your own.

>  **PAGE 85** When you find drawings or images online that appeal to you, try recreating them yourself. Imitating someone else's artwork can be a good way to learn new techniques and fine-tune your own skills. Famous artists have been doing this for centuries. But you don't want to submit copied work as your original idea. See "Copy Rights," on page 85, for more advice about using models.

If you write, go to Jeeves with your questions about poetry, news writing or essays. Ask Jeeves, **Where can I read other kids' work?** You'll find sources of inspiration to fill your blank page—or screen.

>  **PAGE 6** Another way to get ideas is to explore your favorite subjects online. You're most likely to be inspired by the things you truly enjoy. What are your favorite animals or sports? Do you care about a community issue like recycling? Use the search strategies in Chapter 1, "Cast Your Net," to find descriptive sites about your topic.

Publishing on the Net

Now that you've created your masterpiece, why keep it to yourself? Eyes around the world await! With the Internet, you have several ways to share your artistic talents. But first a few basics: If you create artwork offline, you'll need to *digitize* it, or make an electronic image, so it is inside your computer. Depending on your equipment at home or school, you can digitize your work using a *scanner* or you can take a picture of it with a digital camera. If you use a computer graphics program to create your art, then you're all set—your work is already there. Whether you scan an item or create it with your computer, make sure you save it in a format that works with the creative outlet you choose.

Now you're ready to use the following Internet tools to publish your work for the viewing pleasure of others:

👁 E-MAIL IT TO FRIENDS AND FAMILY.

E-mail is the most direct and dependable way to broadcast your creations on the Internet to your personal audience. Send artwork in an attached file or copy it directly into an e-mail, if possible. You can share your work regularly as a sort of e-mail literary or artistic journal. Check out your e-mail application's on-screen help for instructions on attaching files.

👁 CREATE YOUR OWN HOME PAGE.

Your *Internet service provider* (*ISP*) might offer a free *home page* as part of your service package. If so, go to your ISP's *home page* for more details. They'll provide you with instructions on setting it up. You can also go to *http://freezone.com/hpc*. Put your work on your home page, and it will be like having your own Internet gallery!

To create a personal home page, you'll need to *upload* files. Files with pictures or graphics are bigger files than simple word files and will take a bit of time. Also, note the memory capacity of your Web page—often an ISP will set

limits on the amount of content a free Web site can contain.

👁 **SUBMIT YOUR WORK ONLINE.** Some Web sites publish kids' art and writing. When you submit something online, you have to either e-mail it or upload it to a site. Follow the directions. To find sites that accept submissions, ask Jeeves, **Where I can publish my writing online?** or **Where can I share my artwork with other kids?** Visit Kid News at *www.kidnews.com* or the Young Writers Club at *www.cs.bilkent.edu.tr/~david/derya/ywc.html* or Blackberry Creek, the kids' creativity community, at *www.blackberrycreek.com* for more places on the Web to show your stuff. If you use America Online, you can get to Blackberry Creek at keyword **BCreek**.

Poetry in Motion

If beauty is in the eyes of the beholder, then great poetry is in the eyes—and ears—of the audience. Unlike any other written medium, poetry is an expression of the heart, mind, and soul that few other forms can match. But that doesn't mean it has to be all heavy lifting. Some poems are downright light and funny, like this one by Gelett Burgess:

> I never saw a Purple Cow,
> I never hope to see one.
> But I can tell you, anyhow,
> I'd rather see than be one!

Find out how to bring your poetic expressions to life. Ask Jeeves, **Where can I learn how to write poems?**

While you're writing, remember that poetry truly comes to life when it's read aloud. The rhythm and rhyme of words can be like the melody of a song.

Reading your poems out loud can improve your writing. Organize a group poetry reading with one or more friends, or go to *www.favoritepoem.org* to see and hear other people reading their favorite poems.

Internet Encyclopedia

Ask Jeeves to find out about your favorite artist or author. Often he will respond with an option to read a "concise encyclopedia article" about your topic. Be sure to check it out. Jeeves is giving you more than a reference book–type entry; he's giving you a useful brief description of a subject along with a choice of *links*, or *paths*, you can take to other sites of interest.

For instance, ask Jeeves, **Where can I find out about Pablo Picasso?** Not only will you get the brief encyclopedia article about the artist, but you'll also get links to more resources, including an online gallery and detailed background about Picasso's life and work.

Watching Paint Dry

Such is the life of an artist. You work away to mold and shape your creation—in clay, in words, in whatever—send it off to be

reviewed or displayed or published, and then you wait. And wait. And wait. Until, finally, your work finds its way to the eyes of the public (or not).

Getting your work published or viewed, whether online or offline, can seem to take a mighty long time. It can be like watching paint dry—almost impossible. Jeeves recommends that you don't wait around. After you send a piece to one *Web site,* go ahead and send it to another one, or start working on your next creation.

NOTE: Your work might not be used at all. Don't take it personally. Popular Web sites receive lots of items every day, and it's impossible to publish, much less review, every single submission. As in the traditional publishing world, the more places you send your material, the better your chances of getting it picked up.

CHAPTER 10

Seek Advice

If you need help...

- Dealing with friends and family
- Answering a health question
- Solving a problem

Start Here

Some things are personal, and that's the way you want to keep them, thank you. Jeeves won't pry. But maybe he can help you sort things out, if you need to.

Perhaps you've had a fight with a friend. Maybe you feel out of place in school. Or maybe there's nothing wrong at all, but something is on your mind. Some days are like that.

You can get away from it all on the Internet with games, puzzles, music, and gossip about your favorite movie star. Or you can tackle your troubles and discover you're not alone. The World Wide Web awaits. What are you in the mood for?

It doesn't hurt to poke around a little bit and see what a friendly source might have to say about your issue. Have you moved to a new school? Did you lose a pet? Do you have a crush on someone? The Internet can't replace a trusted friend, big sister, or sympathetic grandparent, but you can find valuable support to get you over a bump or answer a pressing question.

Just Ask

Jeeves would be the first to tell you that when it comes to answering questions about the Meaning of Life, you're better off talking with a parent. E-mail your mom or dad if you must! On the other hand, some things you'll discover in your own way over time.

When you have a problem or question about life that you want to learn about online, you can start by simply asking Jeeves a question. For instance, **How do I get rid of a pimple?** Or **How do I take care of my new puppy?** If a specific question doesn't give you the results you need, ask a more general question. For example, **Where can I get information about skin care?** or **How do I take care of my pet?** Jeeves will give you a list of sites that can answer your questions. It's up to you to review the individual sites to see which ones are reliable and can help you most.

PAGE 24 Whether you're searching the Net for personal reasons or for homework help, it's important to choose reliable sources. To find out more, go to Chapter 3, "Consider the Source."

>  Other kids your age are facing the same challenges and may know how to help you with yours, like deciding what to wear to a school dance or getting your coach to let you play in more games. To find out how to hook up with other kids, see Chapter 7, "Make Contact."

Dear Jeeves

Advice columns in newspapers and magazines are very popular because human beings have the need to (1) know we're not alone with our problems and (2) find ways to solve them. You can participate in an online advice column at *www.ajkids.com*. There, kids like you help peers with their problems by exchanging friendly advice and offering a sympathetic ear. Click the ADVICE button to read about the challenges others are having. You can ask for advice yourself or provide an answer if you can relate.

As in all advice columns, not every question and answer can be posted (nor would you want to take the time to read them all!). Check into the advice column from time to time to read the latest postings. Here is a sample:

Dear Jeeves,
My teacher says I am too quiet, and I don't participate verbally. How can I motivate myself to speak more in class?
Sincerely,
M.P.

Jeeves Responds:

Dear M.P.,
Your desire to participate more is wonderful. Set short-term goals for yourself. For the next week, raise your hand at least three times. After a week, modify your goal. Raise your hand and be called on at least three times a day. Progress from there.

Best wishes,
Jeeves

Kids Respond:

Dear M.P.,
If you do not talk in class, you should get to know the people in your class. I kind of have the same problem, so you are not alone. A lot of people are shy, and we are those people. Just try to talk to the people who are in your class and get to know them better. It may make you feel more comfortable.

Best wishes,
Ashley
Age 13
Delaware

Dear M.P.,
I know how you feel because I too had the same problem. I solved it by pretending to be very into class discussions. I began to become more and more involved. Try it.

Sincerely,
Advice Giver
Age 10
Vancouver

Go Ahead and Laugh

When you feel pressure at school or at home, try a laugh to lighten your load. Did you know that just smiling can make you feel better? You don't need to be rolling on the floor to have a good time. Just sit back, relax, and ask Jeeves to do the work. Find out the secret powers of giggles. Ask Jeeves, **Why is laughing good for you?**

Next, get to work on having fun. Track down sites with jokes. Ask Jeeves, **Where can I find jokes for kids?** Share favorite jokes with your family at dinner or e-mail jokes to friends—everyone can use a good laugh!

Perfect Fit

Being in good shape physically and mentally makes you better prepared for life's challenges and allows you to enjoy more activities. Surfing the Internet really can help you stay fit—if you take what you find online and

exercise it in your day-to-day living. Visit *www.kidshealth.org/kid/index.html* to get advice and ideas. Along with other information, you'll find healthy ways to fill your tummy, ways to train for your favorite sport, and ways to mentally relax before a big test.

No Time Like the Present

Often problems simply go away by themselves. But if something is nagging you, you're better off taking care of it sooner rather than later. You don't want to let small problems or issues get to be big ones. That means, if you have an embarrassing question, if someone is not being nice to you, or anything like that, try to get ideas about how to handle it now. Ask Jeeves to help at *www.ajkids.com*. If you're feeling really bad or depressed, or if you're concerned about your safety, turn first to an adult you trust.

Misery Loves Company

You think *you've* got problems... Have you ever noticed that there's always someone worse off than you? When you commiserate, you show sympathy for other people or "share their pain." Commiserating can be a valuable way to help a friend—or seek a friend's help. It shows others you understand what they're going through, whether you're online or offline.

People have troubles with bullies, a new school, a best friend moving away, petty cliques, even serious problems like drug abuse. Whatever the challenge, sometimes helping other people with *their* problems or lending an ear actually makes *your* problems go away. It gives you a different perspective, or outlook, for dealing with your own situation.

 See Chapter 7, "Make Contact," to find out how you can find and maybe commiserate with other kids online.

PART THREE

Jeeves, I Need to Know!

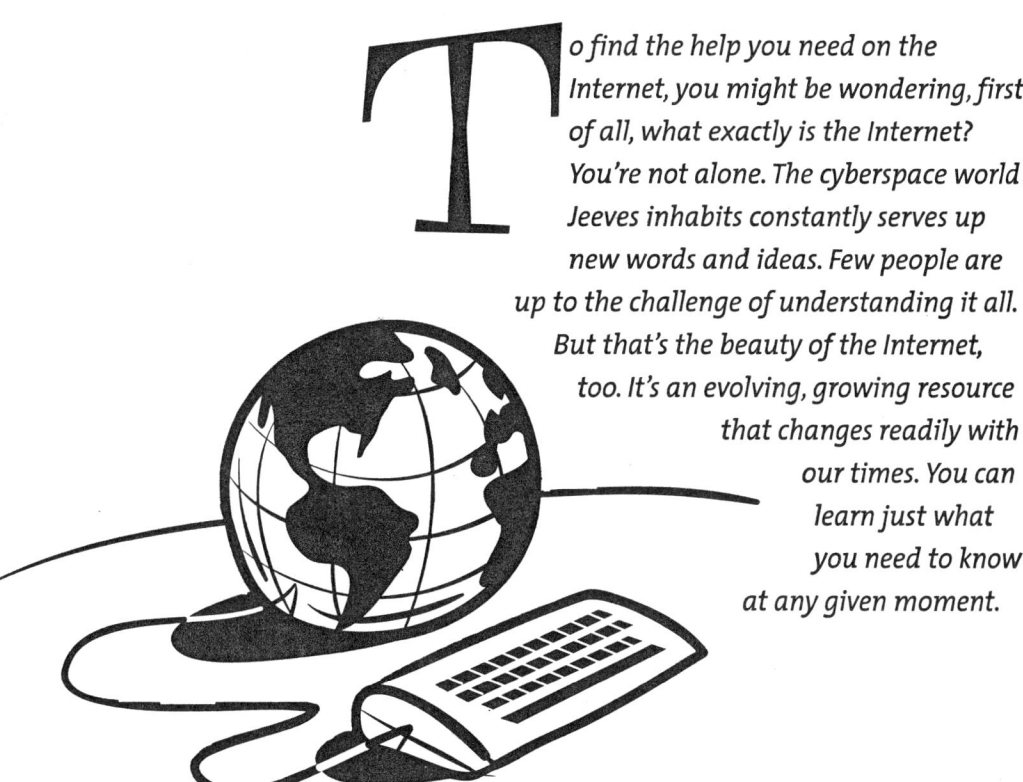

To find the help you need on the Internet, you might be wondering, first of all, what exactly is the Internet? You're not alone. The cyberspace world Jeeves inhabits constantly serves up new words and ideas. Few people are up to the challenge of understanding it all. But that's the beauty of the Internet, too. It's an evolving, growing resource that changes readily with our times. You can learn just what you need to know at any given moment.

The most important way to learn about the Internet is to be an active explorer. Use Jeeves and other resources to work around hurdles and find what you need. Be flexible, determined, and patient, and you will almost always be rewarded by a discovery.

This section gives you the chance to pause before you leap into cyberspace. But you might want to jump inside the Internet to get your bearings first. Go to www.learnthenet.com *and click* Master The Basics. *You'll find drawings that show how the World Wide Web is delivered to your computer—and stories about how it all got started. Read the next section of this book to find out where the trouble spots lie and how you can avoid them. Then look over some of the strange words you'll see along the way in the glossary on page 98. You'll be amazed at how far you can go.*

CHAPTER 11

Search Engines Built for Kids

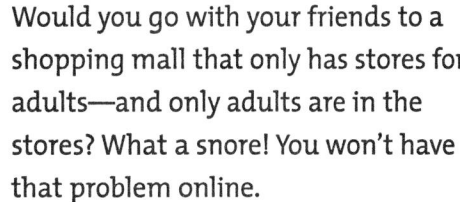

Would you go with your friends to a shopping mall that only has stores for adults—and only adults are in the stores? What a snore! You won't have that problem online.

Search engines created for kids lead you straight to sites designed to appeal to you. There's no need to wade through the world of grown-ups. You've got your own issues to deal with, and really, adult sites (like adults) sometimes just can't relate.

Unlike general search engines, kid search engines are usually *screened*, or *filtered*, to keep in the good stuff that helps you with school and life—and keep out the bad stuff, like pornography, racist propaganda, and other unseemly or upsetting material. Your family can get more information about filtering software at *www.childrenspartnership.org*

At Ask Jeeves for Kids, ***www.ajkids.com***, real people behind the scenes are on the lookout to make sure that the answers Jeeves provides are reliable and appropriate for you. You can expect some TLC. Check out these other search engines designed for kids as well:

> *www.searchopolis.com*
> *www.yahooligans.com*
> *www.lycoszone.com*

If by chance you come across a kid site that seems too babyish for you, just COB! (Click On By!). That's the beauty of browsing!

If you don't find what you're looking for and want to use a general search engine, try ***www.ask.com*** (the grown-up version of Ask Jeeves for Kids) or one of these:

> *www.yahoo.com*
> *www.excite.com*
> *www.webcrawler.com*
> *www.altavista.com*

Use your surfing smarts. Again, think of it as being like shopping in a mall or department store. There are always stores or departments that aren't for kids and aren't worth your time. Click down another aisle and discover something a little more helpful.

CHAPTER 12
Collecting Information

On the Internet, you can gather information in many different ways. As with anything else, though, the more freedom you have, the more responsibility you have, too. Here are a few of the techniques you can use to save information about a topic you're researching and some guidelines for avoiding *plagarism* and staying within the law as you use information you find.

Mark Spots

If you come across a Web site that you think will help you with your homework or a life issue, go ahead and mark it using a tool in your *browser* called *bookmark, favorites,* or *favorite places.* These tools let you leave marks on your Web trail so you can easily go back to certain spots later. Remember to edit your favorites list from time to time to remove sites you no longer need.

Save Pages

To save a page you're visiting so you have a copy on your computer to view offline, go to the FILE menu of your *browser* and select SAVE AS. You will have several choices, depending on the browser you are using. You can save the Web page as TEXT (which saves only the words on the page) or as HTML (which saves the page as it appears on your screen, with images, video, and/or audio). There may be other options as well. Explore the SAVE As function in your browser to find the most useful options for you.

Make sure the page you want to save is active before you use SAVE AS. You can make it active by pointing your cursor and clicking anywhere on the page (don't click a *link*, though, or you will be taken to another Web page!).

In the SAVE AS window, give the file a name that's easy to remember and choose the best place on your hard drive to save it (a place where it will be easy to find later). Then click OK or SAVE.

Copy and Paste

You can copy text from a *Web site* and paste it into another software program, such as a word processing program, to save it for later reference. First, highlight the text you want to copy by dragging your cursor across the text. Go to the EDIT menu and select COPY. Open a page in another program. Then go to the EDIT menu and select PASTE.

When you copy and paste text from a Web site, be sure to copy the *URL* for that Web site and paste it into the same file. Also, read the ABOUT or BACKGROUND section for the Web site and copy and paste information about the publisher. Collect all the information you will need to cite your source properly for a school project bibliography (see page 28) or return to the page if you need to.

Copy Rights

With today's technology, you have the ability to copy just about anything you find on the Internet. But you don't necessarily have the right to use it in any way you want to.

Material on the Internet, just like material in books and magazines, is protected by *copyright* laws. These laws make it illegal for others to use the material in certain ways without permission. If you *scroll* down to the bottom of a Web page, you'll usually see a copyright notice that includes the letter "c" in a circle and a date, followed by the name of a person or company. Check the beginning pages of this book, and you'll see the copyright notice that protects its contents. The name shows who owns the copyright. Sometimes the owner is the creator of the work. Sometimes the owner is someone else.

Many Web sites also have a *link* to a copyright page describing their rights. The copyright page may describe how the material can be used, but it can be hard to understand copyright pages because they're written in legal language. It's okay to use other people's work in your own personal projects—for example, you can copy a poem into your personal journal or put it in a letter to a friend. It's also okay to use excerpts (small portions) of published materials in a school report, as long as you give the author or artist credit. But if you *publish* your journal or report—online or offline—you must have permission to include someone else's copyrighted material.

If you don't give the creator credit when you use their material in a school project, that's *plagarism*.

Plagarism is stealing, and most teachers consider it a serious offense. So don't forget to cite your sources!

Did you know that you're a copyright owner, too? Anything you have written—even your poetry or journal—is protected by copyright from the moment you put the words together. Copyright notices are intended to prevent others from taking your work and selling it as their own.

If you have questions about using material you find online, e-mail the site directly. There is usually an e-mail link next to the copyright information at the bottom of a Web site's *home page*. Or look for a CONTACT US link on the main page. If you want more information, ask Jeeves, **Where can I learn more about copyrights?**

PAGE 24

For schoolwork, you can quote someone else's words or use their ideas if you credit them. See Chapter 3, "Consider the Source," for tips on citing your sources.

86

CHAPTER 13
Follow the Peas and Cues (or Netiquette)

Just like any other group of people who get together, people on the Internet follow rules of behavior that are accepted—and enforced—by one another. The code of online conduct is called *netiquette*.

The last thing you want to do is get into a *flame* war or SHOUT at someone in a *chat room*. The repercussions will be instant and brutal. Everyone in a chat room will let you know you stepped over the line. And Web site monitors might boot you off their site for good.

Follow these guidelines to avoid embarrassment and show some Web savvy:

- Before you join a discussion board or other online forum, read the *community's FAQs*, or *frequently asked questions*. The FAQs get you up to speed so you don't ask questions that the group discussed long ago.

- Be considerate. Add your two cents' worth only when you have something to say. Don't send off-topic or off-color messages, or you will be *flamed* by other participants. That is, someone will likely let you know through a harsh or embarrassing e-mail that you're out of line.

- On the other hand, sometimes a user will lob *flame-bait* (Internet lingo for an insulting message) into a discussion just to get an angry exchange going. Ignore it and keep your head above the fray.

- Using all uppercase letters LIKE THIS is considered shouting on the Internet and will be a dead giveaway that you are either a clod or a clueless beginner. It's best not to shout.

- Every online *community* or *chat room* has its own style or personality. If what you see doesn't appeal to you, just leave. Just as you do when picking your friends at school, stick with online communities you respect.

CHAPTER 14

Safety Net: Protect Yourself While Surfing

What's the big deal about all this safety stuff? The way adults carry on, you would think pirates were stalking cyberspace to cart away treasures of names, addresses, birthdays, and anything else they can get their hands on to sell it on the black market. Or that professional thieves were waiting to steal your information in order to impersonate you and run up charges at shopping *Web sites*. Well, actually, this is pretty close to the truth. Bad things are happening to unknowing users of the Internet. The good news is that, by taking a few simple precautions, you can make sure none of these things happen to *you*.

Private Practices

You've got a name, likes, dislikes, experiences, ideas. Let's face it—you've got a whole self and you don't want just anybody knowing every detail about you. Much less for them to sell the information to someone else, who may wind up harassing you by sending you annoying e-mails, or *spamming* you.

Privacy is one of the most treasured rights in a democracy. It means that your identity and all the details about your life belong to you. Privacy laws protect that right. Privacy also means safety, especially for kids. The fact is, there are dangerous people on the Internet, and you really don't want them to know where you live or how to call you. The U.S. Federal Trade Commission (FTC) suggests you follow these guidelines to keep your privacy to yourself, so to speak:

- Don't give out your last or family name, your home address, or your phone number in *chat rooms*, on *discussion boards*, or to online pen pals. Don't tell other kids—or adults—your screen name, user ID, or password.

- Kid Web sites are required by law to make their *privacy policies* public. Talk with your parents about the policies at the sites you visit so that you all know what information is being collected about you and what each site does with the information.

- Sites are not supposed to collect more information than necessary for the activity you want to participate in. You should be able to participate in many activities online without having to give out any information about yourself.

- If a site makes you uncomfortable or asks for more information than you want to share, leave the site. Note that Web sites must get your parent's permission before they collect many kinds of information from you.

- Surf the Internet with your parents when you can. Besides teaching them what you know, you can get ideas about what they think is trustworthy. If you don't surf with your parents, talk to them about the sites you're visiting.

- If a Web site has information about you that you and a parent don't want it to have, your parent can ask to see the information and then have the Web site delete it.

For more advice about privacy online and how to take action when you feel your rights have been violated, visit *www.getnetwise.org* or the FTC Web site for kids at *www.ftc.gov/bcp/conline/edcams/kidzprivacy/index.html*

Internet Rx

Though they may seem harmless enough, your Internet travels can expose you to all kinds of viruses and

vermin. That's because some of the Internet's best features can also be the most dangerous: Anyone can access the Internet and hide behind a fake identity.

You don't want to let someone ruin your online experience by being rude, crude, destructive, scary, or violent. Using your head—and your mouse—you can create a safety net that protects you and still leaves loads of room for fun.

Here's an online preventive prescription especially for kids, inspired by Lawrence Magid, founder of SafeKids.com. For more information, visit *www.safekids.com*

1. Ask a parent, sibling, or friend to join you.
2. Stand up together in front of your computer and spin around in a circle three times. (Try not to bump into each other when you get dizzy!)
3. Say these statements out loud, together. You can sing or rap the words if you want.

"My name, user ID, password, address, phone number, e-mail address, age, school name and location, and any other information about me shall never be given to anyone over the Internet unless my parents and I agree it's a good idea."

"I'll never plan to meet alone and in person someone I meet online, because I know that it can be dangerous."

"If someone sends me a message that is threatening or makes me feel uncomfortable, I will not respond to it, but instead will show it to a parent or teacher immediately so they can handle it."

"My parents and I will agree together what can be downloaded from a Web site, so we can avoid viruses and so we know the download works with my computer."

"I agree to talk with my parents about what I see and do online because I know that they can learn a thing or two from me and because they can help me if something bad happens."

4. Now do the secret handshake. (It's your secret handshake, so you can make this part up on your own.)
5. Celebrate! Surf to your heart's content.

Jeeves takes Internet safety seriously, and you should, too. Make your safety net even stronger by asking Jeeves, **Where can I learn about Internet safety?**

Virus Protection

A computer *virus* is a computer program that can do damage to your computer files or cause your computer to automatically do something you don't want—such as send an e-mail to everyone on your e-mail address list.

Viruses are passed from one computer to another through *downloads*, *uploads*, and e-mails. It's a good idea to have a virus protection program installed on your computer before you go online. You will also need to keep the program updated by downloading the latest version—from the company that makes the program's *Web site* or from your *ISP*. The latest version will protect you from the latest viruses.

To avoid getting a virus in the first place, never download a file unless you know the person who sent it and you are sure you know exactly what it is. If you're not sure, write to the person and ask what the file is before downloading.

CHAPTER 15

How to Can Spam

Spam, or junk e-mail, is unwanted mail that is deceitful, misleading, offensive, or just annoying because you did not give your permission to receive it. Or you gave your permission but didn't realize you were giving it. Spam can take the form of chain letters, advertisements, money-making schemes, and every other imaginable come-on that can be put into an e-mail message.

How do you become a spam target in the first place? As soon as you start giving your e-mail address to businesses and people you don't know—online or offline—you will more than likely start receiving spam. If you *register* to use services at a *Web site* and provide your e-mail address, your address could be used for marketing and other advertisements. Also, your own *browser* could be giving your e-mail address away as it communicates with Web sites you visit.

Spam is universally disliked, even as marketers and pranksters cheaply send out more and more of it all the time. Here are some ways to fight back:

PROTECT YOUR ADDRESS. Your e-mail address is your personal ID. It's against the law for a Web site to ask for your e-mail address without a parent's or guardian's consent if you are under 18 years old. One way to protect your e-mail address is to change your preference setting in your browser software. If you use Netscape Communicator™, go to the EDIT menu and select PREFERENCES. Click ADVANCED on the left side of the screen. If there's a checkmark in the box beside the statement "Send e-mail address as anonymous FTP password," click the box to remove the checkmark.

OPT OUT. Many Web sites require you to *opt out*, or contact them specifically to take your name off an e-mail list. You may automatically receive a site's junk mail unless you check a box that says you do not want to receive it. Often, to opt out, you will have to write to a particular e-mail address or visit a certain Web page and search through the contents to find the place where you can request that you be removed from the list.

READ THE FINE PRINT. Check a Web site's *privacy policy* to find out what it will do with your information. Such statements are usually easy to find on a *home page*. But they aren't always easy to understand—even for computer professionals. If you don't find a privacy statement or don't understand the one that's there, think twice before you become a regular visitor to that site.

Find out more about your right to privacy online in "Privacy Practices." (PAGE 90)

👁 **FILTER IT OUT.** Most e-mail programs offer settings to *screen*, or *filter*, your e-mails before they arrive in your mailbox. The process is very simple. Just take a moment to check the HELP feature of your e-mail program to find out how to set it up. Like a personal secretary, the software will do the screening work for you. Because spammers often change their e-mail address to get around filters, you'll need to update your filters frequently.

👁 **TRASH IT FIRST.** You can usually tell when an e-mail is spam before you even open it. The subject or title bar may have a silly come-on like "Win a Free Trip!" or "Make Money Online!" You may not recognize the sender of the e-mail. But look out! Spammers are getting more creative about e-mail subjects and sender names, making them sound friendly and appealing. Your motto can be "When in doubt, toss it out," just as you would toss food in the refrigerator you think might be spoiled.

👁 **DO NOT RESPOND.** If you e-mail the spammer back to ask them to take you off their list, they'll know

you actually exist and that the e-mail address they have for you is valid. You'll just get more spam when they add you to other lists.

- 👁 **REPORT SPAM TO YOUR ISP.** Check out your *Internet service provider's (ISP's)* spam policy by visiting its *home page* or calling the customer support line. Often the process is as simple as forwarding the spam to a particular e-mail address.

- 👁 **NOTIFY AN ADULT.** If you receive a threat, abusive prank, or creepy e-mail from anyone, notify a parent, caregiver, or teacher immediately. If the harassment persists or seems dangerous, contact your local police department.

Software and Web technology changes every day, so check out the home page of your ISP every few months to take advantage of their updated suggestions for protecting your e-mail address and combating spam. For more ideas, ask Jeeves, **What can I do about spam?**

GLOSSARY

On Your Terms

You may not think of these strange-sounding Internet words as your terms at all. Most of them were made up by and for computer programmers—not for kids. But it's still a good idea to *make* them your terms. Learning Internet lingo will help you do things your way on the Net.

Application — A computer program that helps you perform a certain function on your computer. E-mail, word processing, and browser programs are examples of applications.

Archive — Information or material, such as frequently asked questions or past photographs, that is collected over time and stored in one place where people can refer to it.

Audio — Any sound, such as music, special effects, and narrations.

Bandwidth — The capacity an Internet connection can carry at one time. A high bandwidth means that a Web site, especially one with animations and audio, will load more quickly on your screen.

Blocking — A service available with some browsers and Internet service providers that allows parents to block access to certain Web sites.

Bookmark — A Netscape Navigator and Communicator tool that saves places for you on the Web so you can easily go back to them. When Netscape is open to a Web page you want to mark, go to the BOOKMARKS menu and select ADD BOOKMARKS. Your bookmarks are collected in the same menu on the menu bar. For more tips on working with bookmarks, see Netscape's Help tool.

Browser — An application that you use to view Web sites on the Internet. Netscape's Navigator and Microsoft's Internet Explorer are examples of browsers.

Chat or live chat — A way of communicating with a person or a group online by typing messages instead of talking. Online chats take place in chat rooms and happen in real time—that is, messages are seen immediately.

Clip art — Drawings or pictures that you can download or copy and paste into your homework assignments, e-journal, and so on.

Community — On the Internet, refers to the regular members, audience, or users of a Web site's services or forums.

Cookie — The name for a piece of information placed in your browser software by a Web site you visit. Anytime you register at a site, cookies are added to your browser. Cookies enable Web sites to offer you personalized Web pages. They also allow a Web site to tag you and track your travels on the Internet. You can prevent Web sites from attaching cookies to your browser by changing the preferences in your browser software.

Copyright — The legal right to reproduce, publish, and sell an original work such as a poem, drawing, story, painting, news article, film, or book. Only the copyright owner has this right. Everyone else must get permission to use the material in these ways.

Cyberspace — The universe of wires, computers, and digital information that make up the Internet. The prefix cyber- refers to automatic systems and processes.

Digitize — To electronically scan a drawing or photograph so that you have a copy of it saved on your computer. Digitized images can be saved on a disk, uploaded to a Web site, or e-mailed to a friend.

Discussion board — See Message board.

Domain name — The part of a Web site address that describes the owner of that site. For example, *ajkids.com* is the Ask Jeeves for Kids domain name.

Download — Copying an item from a remote computer onto your computer. You can download music, photographs, computer programs, and more. Usually you will have to choose the folder on your computer where you want to save the downloaded file. See also Upload.

E-mail — An electronic mail message sent over a computer network, such as the Internet.

FAQs — Frequently Asked Questions. Many Web sites provide answers to a list of common questions to help visitors get answers quickly.

Favorite Places — An America Online (AOL) tool that saves Web pages so you can easily go back to them. When AOL is open to a Web page you want to save, simply click the heart in the corner of the page. To go back to the page later, click on the FAVORITES menu and drag down the list to the page you want. It's also possible to send pages in your Favorite Places list to others via e-mail. See AOL's Help tool for tips on working with Favorite Places.

Favorites — A Microsoft Internet Explorer tool that saves Web pages for you so you can easily go back to them. When Explorer is open to a Web page you want to mark, go to the FAVORITES menu and select ADD TO FAVORITES. Your favorites are collected in the same menu on the menu bar. For more tips on working with Favorites, see Explorer's Help tool.

Filter — A tool offered in some computer programs that organizes, and often blocks, information available on the Internet, enabling users to prevent kids from going to inappropriate sites.

Flame, fame-bait — To send an angry or crude message in e-mail or during a chat session in an attempt to provoke an angry reaction and start a flame war. The best way to handle flame-baiting is simply to ignore it.

FTP — File Transfer Protocol. A method for sending files between computers on the Internet.

Graphics — Photographs, cartoons, illustrations, and other visual elements.

Help — Instructions to guide you in using a program or a Web site's services. Most Web sites that offer a service also offer online help. A HELP button or text link on a home page will take you to another page for the instructions. Always look over a site's online help when you first visit—you can find tips and tricks to make your experience even better.

Home page or home — The main page of a Web site, similar to the front page of a newspaper. Your home page is also the Web page your browser goes to when you open your browser program. With some browsers, you can choose your home page.

Host — A computer at another location that stores, or hosts, a Web site. Many Internet service providers (ISPs) offer to host personalized Web pages for their customers. See also Server.

HTML — Hypertext Markup Language. The common software programming language for creating sites on the World Wide Web. Most Web site addresses end with *.html* or *.htm*.

HTTP — Hypertext Transfer Protocol. The common communications language for computers to interact on the World Wide Web and the basis for all Web site addresses. All Internet addresses start with the prefix *http://*. Usually (though not always) the letters *www* follow.

Icon — A graphic or thumbnail-size image. If you roll your mouse pointer over an icon and the pointer becomes a hand, that means the icon is also a link and clicking it will take you to a related Web page. For example, an icon that shows a question mark in a box will probably take you to the site's Help page.

Instant message — A note that goes directly from you to the receiver without the time delay of regular e-mail. It can be typed or recorded using a special service offered by Internet service provider America Online (AOL). Check with your ISP for similar services.

Internet — An international network of electronically connected computers. Also called the Net. See also World Wide Web.

ISP — Internet Service Provider. Your ISP links your computer, via cable or phone lines, to the Internet for a certain fee. America Online and Earthlink are examples of ISPs.

Keyword – Sometimes also written as key word. Keywords are words used to describe an idea, person, or thing that you are searching for on the Internet. A keyword search is an Internet search using keywords.

Link — Words or items that are highlighted with an underline or different color. When you click a link, you are taken to another Web page about the highlighted word or item.

Live chat — See Chat.

Load — The transferring of graphics and words making up a Web site. When you visit a site, the items are loaded onto your screen.

Login or logon — To connect to the Internet or to sign in or register at a Web site.

Mailing list — An organization's e-mail list for sending out material—such as material for group discussion, a newsletter, or advertisements. When you put your e-mail address on a mailing list, you'll receive e-mails at any time, and you can respond to the list if you wish. NOTE: Joining a mailing list may mean you will receive more spam (junk e-mail).

Matching question — A related question that comes up when you ask Jeeves a question at *www.ajkids.com*. You pick the best matching question for what you want to know.

Message board — An area on a Web site where users can post comments and read the comments of others.

Metasearch results — Answers found by search engines other than the one you're using. For example, when you ask Jeeves a question at *www.ajkids.com*, he will bring back results from other search engines, such as Education World, as well as matching questions (see above). Metasearch results make it possible for you to use more than one search engine at the same time.

Modem — A device that works like a telephone to call up and connect your computer with another computer, such as your ISP.

Multimedia — A combination of media, such as animation and sound.

Net — See Internet.

Netiquette — Informal but widely accepted common courtesies and standards of behavior on the Net.

Offline — Disconnected from the Internet, or an activity that takes place off the Internet.

Online — Connected to the Internet, or an activity that takes place on the Internet.

Opt out — To inform a Web site that you do not want to be on its mass e-mailing list, usually by removing a checkmark from a box or by sending an e-mail notice. Registering for a site's services, purchasing an item through a site, or even just visiting a site puts you on such lists.

Path — The step-by-step trail from one Web page to another. On the Web, you can travel a path by clicking on one link after another. See also Link.

Personal page — A Web page that offers custom information chosen by the user. This service is offered by Ask Jeeves at *www.ask.com* and by other Web sites.

Player — A software feature, or plug-in, that enables your browser to show videos or play audio files offered by a Web site. See also Plug-in.

Plagarism — Stealing someone else's idea, writing, or artwork and passing it off as your own.

Plug-in — Software that enables an existing application to play audio, video, or other multimedia features at a Web site. Plug-ins can usually be downloaded for free. If you visit a Web site that requires a plug-in to view its contents, the site will prompt you to download the plug-in if you don't already have it.

Portal — A Web site that serves as your entrance to the World Wide Web by offering searches, news, and "channels" for sports, health, and other special interests, as well as other services.

Privacy policy — Usually found on a Web site's home page, their privacy policy explains what information the site collects from visitors and what they will do with that information.

Q&A site — Question-and-Answer site. A Web site that answers questions for users, such as reference questions related to your homework.

Registering — Kids are required to register at some Web sites in order to participate in activities like chats and message boards or to sign up for services like a Personal page. Registration usually involves getting your parents' permission. It is important to get your parents' assistance when registering at a site, even if parental approval is not required, so they can help you choose what information to give out.

Results — A list of Web sites found by your search engine in response to a question or keywords you submit. On keyword search engines, search results appear in a list with descriptions of the Web sites found so you can choose the sites most suitable for your needs. Click the results link to go to the corresponding Web site.

Scanner — A device that allows you to digitize (make an electronic copy of) something, such as a photograph, illustration, or other graphic, so you can store it on your computer. The word scan also describes the practice of reviewing a document or Web site to get an impression of its contents.

Screen or prescreen — To review Web pages to see if they fit your purpose. When you ask a question at *www.ajkids.com*, Jeeves responds with Web pages that have been prescreened by Ask Jeeves editors. See also Filter.

Scroll — To move a Web page up, down, or sideways by clicking on the scroll bar. With limited space available on your computer screen, it's a good idea to scroll until you have seen the entire contents of a Web page. Otherwise, you might miss something.

Search — To look for something on the World Wide Web. When you type in a question at *www.ajkids.com*, Jeeves searches the Web to find the answer and brings back links to Web pages.

Search engine — Software that skims the World Wide Web to find the information you ask for. Ask Jeeves for Kids is a search engine that responds to a question you submit. Searchopolis is a search engine that responds to keywords you submit. Search engines provide their services for free on the World Wide Web.

Server — A computer that hosts or stores data, such as the data that makes up a Web site, and gives remote computers like yours access to that data. You access the information using your browser and a Web site address, or URL.

Site map or site index — An index or table of contents for a Web site that has links to the items listed. Many Web site home pages offer site maps through a text or icon link. Site maps are a good way to review quickly whether a site can meet your needs.

Spam — Spam is no longer just the name of a canned meat product. Now it's the Internet word for unwanted or junk e-mail.

Surf — To search for and review Web sites and otherwise explore the World Wide Web.

Upload — To send a copy of an item from your computer to a remote computer.

You can upload art submissions to a Web site, for example. See also Download.

URL — Uniform Resource Locator. An address that allows your computer to find a Web site on a server, or remote computer.

Video — Moving images or animation.

Virus — Damaging computer code that can be passed from one computer to another through downloads, uploads, and e-mails. It's a good idea to have a virus protection program installed on your computer before you go online.

Web — See World Wide Web.

Web page — Just as a book is made up of pages, a Web site is made up of Web pages, which are individual screens of information.

Web site — If the World Wide Web is like a library, then a Web site is like a book. A Web site address, or URL, is similar to a book's library catalog number.

Web site address — The information your browser needs to locate a Web site. See also URL.

World Wide Web or Web or www — A network on the Internet that enables the use of graphics, sound, video, links, and other interactive elements to present a visually engaging online experience. See also Internet.

AUTHOR CALLIE GREGORY is an educational writer and multimedia content developer who first turned to Jeeves to help her find answers in a pinch. Her favorite question for Jeeves: Is the moon made of cheese? She is the author of Ask Jeeves' first book for kids, *Jeeves, I'm Bored: 25 Internet Adventures for Kids*. She has written publications and developed interactive products for teachers and kids for Scholastic Inc., Dorling Kindersley, and Tribune Corp., among others. Callie lives in Sunnyvale, CA.

CONSULTANT LYNDA GREENE has had a distinguished career in education that rivals even the exploits of Jeeves. She has served as a classroom teacher, a reading specialist, and a teacher trainer. She managed education at The Tech Museum of Innovation in San Jose, CA, and directed the School Collaborative Program at Stanford University. She has managed product development for Scholastic Inc. and Tribune Corp. and advises school districts and corporations. Lynda lives in Menlo Park, CA.

ILLUSTRATOR MARCOS SORENSEN draws Jeeves and works as an art director at Ask Jeeves. His drawings have appeared in many magazines—*Time, Sports Illustrated, Discover,* and *Wired* to name a few. He has also worked for companies like Coca Cola, Sega, MTV, and Cartoon Network, and has even designed two monster Swatch watches. Marcos was born in Mexico, raised in Canada, and currently lives in San Francisco.